THE 4MM WAGON

PART ONE Opens, Minerals and Hoppers

by GEOFF KENT

WILD SWAN PUBLICATIONS LTD.

"90% of the average steam age goods train consisted of minerals, opens and vans . . . " 8F No. 48129 ambles up the West Coast main line at Dallam, Warrington on 3rd July 1965.
AUTHOR

Designed by Paul Karau
Printed by Amadeus Press, Huddersfield

Published by
WILD SWAN PUBLICATIONS LTD
1—3 Hagbourne Road, Didcot, Oxon OX11 8DP

Title page: *An interesting selection of wagons in this glimpse of Stoke Gifford yard, south side, on 25th June 1951. Nearest the camera is a Ministry of Transport steel mineral, apparently still in original bauxite livery. Of riveted construction, with pressed steel end and side doors, and bottom doors but no top flaps, this design became BR Diagram 1/103. To its right the ex-private owner with seven-plank sides is a pre-1923 12-tonner with part of the name still vaguely legible; the grease axleboxes and only one wide top plank, rather than two, distinguish it from the later standard design. Next to it is a wooden loco coal wagon with unusual vertical ironwork, probably of LMS constituent origin. Beyond it, and in the distance, are GWR ballast wagons, and beyond that a standard GWR end-verandah brake van. The roofs of at least two more are visible among the lines of vans, which include representatives from each of the Big Four. LMS vehicles with sliding doors and roof vents predominate, but both planked and plywood GWR vans with hinged doors can be seen, together with a vertically-planked LNER example with sliding doors, and, towards the top left of the picture, the distinctive three-arc roof outline of a typical Southern van.*
ROYE ENGLAND

INTRODUCTION

On the face of it, just another pannier tank on another local goods train. But just look at the variety of wagons behind it – 20-odd, plus a brake, and hardly two the same. And yet they are all just common-or-garden wagons, haphazardly marshalled in the manner typical of pick-up or transfer goods workings. This photograph was taken near Twyford on 20th November 1948.   J. F. RUSSELL-SMITH

Despite the valiant efforts over the years of a number of extremely knowledgeable and talented people, goods wagons have tended to remain the poor relation of the model railway world. While endless skill is lavished upon coaches, track, buildings and especially engines, the rich, but often subtle variety of goods wagon types and designs gets surprisingly little attention. I say surprisingly because freight was and is, after all, the bread and butter traffic of the railways in most areas, and the number and variety of goods vehicles has always vastly outweighed the number of passenger-carrying ones.

It is surprising too, because information on both the prototype and the techniques of reproducing it in miniature is not lacking. Perhaps the clue lies in the apparent sameness of the more common goods wagons: 90% of the average steam-age goods train consisted of minerals, opens and vans, and it may be significant that to inject a little variety people seem to concentrate on private-owner wagons (which admittedly were very numerous until the fifties), and private-owner vans (which were anything but), together with more than the usual sprinkling of special-purpose types like glass carriers and weltrols. In this they have been aided and abetted by manufacturers of ready-to-run equipment and, in some cases, kits as well, who, understandably perhaps, have favoured the colourful and the arcane against the drab and the commonplace, which no doubt boosted sales but did little to encourage the accurate representation of typical goods trains, which, curiously enough, did not generally consist of odd,

picturesquely-liveried vehicles belonging to a dozen different owners from all points of the compass.

But it isn't my intention to enlarge upon the subject of private-owner vehicles, at least not in the period of their heyday. Anyone who wishes to study that subject can do no better than to read Chris Crofts' scholarly treatise in past numbers of the *Model Railway Journal*, coupled with Bill Hudson's albums of photographs. Nor am I qualified to discourse at length on early goods vehicles, although, having said that, the basic four-wheeled wagon did not change much in essence throughout the steam era; the vehicles built by British Railways in the first ten years of its existence are quite recognisably descended from those built a hundred years before. By contrast, the changes that have taken place in the last quarter of a century have been far more dramatic, with wagons of advanced design, a return to colourful private-owner liveries, and the virtual elimination of the traditional short-wheelbased, low-capacity vehicles of yesteryear.

Regrettably, perhaps, the period of my closest acquaintance with the original, and of my experience of reproducing it in miniature, coincides with the time when wagon liveries were for the most part at their least inspiring. From 1948 the bulk of the wagon fleet was either bauxite brown for vacuum-fitted and piped stock or pale grey for unfitted vehicles. In service these stimulating colours quickly degenerated to cheerless shades of rust, muck and unpainted wood, thus becoming incidentally far more difficult to reproduce successfully – further reasons, perhaps, for many modellers' preference for the Golden Age of railways. Even so, the apparently common assumption that the efforts that went into maintaining the gleaming brass and spotless paintwork of locomotives and carriages ever extended to the humble goods wagon is rather misplaced; goods vehicles were usually dirty, never cleaned externally, and frequently scarred by misuse.

It is something of a paradox, however, that the years which saw wagon liveries at their least colourful were also those of just about the greatest variety of wagon types. Remaining pre-and early post-grouping vehicles (in many cases all-wooden) rubbed shoulders with the standard designs of the Big Four, who had gradually diversified into steel and plywood as alternative construction materials. These in turn ran cheek-by-jowl with British Railways' developments of these traditional designs and the early forerunners of today's hi-tech vehicles, as the railways fought by greater specialisation to attract new traffics that demanded faster and more efficient handling, and to retain old ones for which road transport was an ever more competitive option. The results were all-too-often a short-lived compromise, but served to increase still further the range of vehicles to be seen. Piecemeal modifications to existing vehicles, and design changes in newer batches of established types generated even more variety. And if you take into account the hundred-and-one minor variations in such things as brakes, axleboxes and lettering, it is rather to be wondered at that any mixed goods train could ever have contained two identical vehicles.

The problem remains that for all these differences, a train of, say, 13-ton high-sided open wagons is still a train of virtually indistinguishable vehicles, especially if they are all nominally the same colour. You need to look pretty closely to tell a Southern Railway open from a Great Western one, or an early BR Lowfit from an LNER one, or for that matter an LMS cattle van from its Midland predecessor, and at first glance you may not be able to tell them apart. For this reason it's quite understandable that many modellers are going to be less than totally fascinated by the minutiae of wagon design, and will content themselves with putting kits together straight out of the box, rather than spending valuable time studying ways in which they can be adapted to produce a wider range of related, and often, frankly, not very dissimilar types.

My intention, therefore, in the following pages is threefold: first, to outline the construction of a selection of kits more or less as the manufacturers intended, covering as wide a field of materials as possible. Second, to assist those who are looking to broaden the scope of their wagon fleet by suggesting ways in which some of those same kits can be modified by judicious butchery and modest scratchbuilding. And third, by more extensive scratchbuilding, to produce types of vehicle which are so far poorly represented in either kit or ready-to-run form.

Wagons to be considered will all have been built in the period 1900–1960, and mostly post-1923, since this fits in with my own chosen modelling period of the mid-to-late fifties. This, I'm afraid, automatically tends to reduce, or even eliminate the representation of some manufacturers' production, namely those whose kits are largely confined to pre-grouping types: Model Wagon Co., Slaters, D&S and

Coopercraft all fit into this category, and I apologise now to anyone who feels slighted as a result. But many of the techniques used will apply to earlier and later vehicles, just as the technology of wagon-building itself made only gradual advances until quite recently.

I should also make the point that some of the models described have been built over a period of some years, and the kits and proprietary items involved may not in all cases still be available, or may be marketed under another name. The history of Airfix kits and ready-to-run products, together with Mainline, and their various inheritors, becomes quite involved, as does the saga of the dynasty that began with Ian Kirk's 'basic kits' in the 1970s. The same applies to small parts manufacturers, and if at times the reader becomes confused, I can only plead that, as a consumer

outside the trade, I do too. And although I think I have a fair grasp of the overall picture of 4mm scale kits and bits, I can't claim to know every manufacturer's range backwards, and there are sure to be things available of which I'm blissfully unaware. In any case, it's a constantly changing picture, so anything I say today might well not be true tomorrow.

With these provisos, my aim will be to produce a representative range of wagon types, such as might be seen in the average pick-up goods of the period. As far as possible I shall try to avoid regional variations, but you may find odd references to the railways around Wrexham, since some of the wagons have been built to suit the long-term objective of a layout somewhere on the Shrewsbury & Chester line in Western Region days. I shall also steer clear of vehicles which would only, or mainly, be seen in full trainloads (steel

coil wagons and iron ore tipplers, for instance), together with one-offs or types with very limited working patterns. But when it comes to variety, a mixed goods *might* include almost anything, and some of the less usual, but still quite numerous types are fair game: pallet brick wagons, for example (over 1400 built), steel-bodied bulk grain vans (827 built in all by the GWR, the LMS and BR) or Conflat L's (2,242).

But whether you're building kits straight out of the box or seeking to introduce a bit of individuality by constructing variations on a theme, background information is indispensable. There are few kits indeed which answer in their instructions all the queries the builder is likely to have, whether he is an apprentice or a time-served craftsman. Livery details are often sketchy, and you will search in vain

Anyone who thinks goods wagons are all the same should study this picture, taken at Norton Junction marshalling yard on 6th June 1953. Apart from the odd van and bogie bolster, the yard is crammed with open and mineral wagons of all shapes and sizes.
F. W. SHUTTLEWORTH

The variety of traffic in this fascinating picture taken in the mid-1950s is surely enough to whet anyone's appetite. And yet, with only a few exceptions, almost all the wagons you can see are vans, opens and minerals. There are a few containers on conflats, some empty horse-boxes, a rail-mounted crane, a plate wagon and a handful of bolsters, and one or two specialised vans like the banana van on the right — perhaps fifteen or twenty out of what must be hundreds of very ordinary wagons. But if the rest seem undistinguished, just compare the two wooden-bodied minerals in the foreground, or the two on the right above the banana van, or the three opens in front of it. The differences are subtle, but they're there all the same. AUTHOR'S COLLECTION

as a rule for guidance as to possible variations in detail, let alone in other batches of similar wagons. Occasionally the information is downright misleading.

Unfortunately, the days are gone when you could pop down to the local goods yard and observe at first hand details of the wagon stock, which might range from the latest vacuum-filled pallet van (state-of-the-art in 1960) to a pre-group, or even Victorian survivor put out to grass as a stationary stores van against the blocks in the furthest corner of the depot. Even as recently as the early eighties, there was still a tremendous variety of wagons of traditional design in departmental use, while internal-user fleets on privately-owned works sidings offered numerous gems of former revenue-earning types pensioned off decades previously. The lucky few have been saved for posterity on preserved lines, but even these organisations have tended to look askance at anything built in the last fifty years or so that can't be adorned with a private-owner livery or two-foot-high letters proclaiming the identity of one of the Big Four railways or their constituents.

Nowadays, the chances of finding more than an odd one or two vehicles of traditional style on their wheels are slim indeed, and even these are likely to be of BR build. Even the familiar grounded van body is nearly a thing of the past, at least on railway property, though a safari round the farmyards in almost any part of the country can still produce something of interest. My own small village can boast vans of NB, GE and GC (actually MS&L!) origin, all in quite reasonable repair – certainly good enough for detailed measurements to be taken, given the (sometimes rather bemused) agreement of the owner. While all such grounded stores are vans of one sort or another, the range is really enormous, the only common denominator being the possession of a roof. So while ordinary box vans predominate, you can see horse boxes, cattle vans, brake vans, fish vans, meat vans, containers – you name it, there's one somewhere.

All the same, the most readily accessible sources of information are in published form. I shall include a selective bibliography at the end of Volume 2, selective because it will list only the books that I have personally found useful in pursuing my own interests. Even so, some gaps remain: the definitive book on Southern Railway wagons is still waiting to be published, for example. If you have access to past numbers of the various model railway magazines you will find a huge range of drawings and articles available to you, though you may have to go back to the fifties to get anything like a complete picture. Unfortunately, the BR/OPC service of copies of original works drawings seems to have fallen by the wayside; a great pity, since the scope was truly monumental and the service first class. You were hard to please if you couldn't find what you were looking for here, the only problem being the difficulty of pinpointing it from the often sparse description in the catalogues.

Finally in this introduction, I think I ought to make a few points about some aspects of my style of wagon construction. I try to model the body as faithfully as possible in most respects, but I have to admit to a few short-cuts here and there in the underframe department. Working on the premise that if you can't see it on a photograph of the original you're unlikely to miss it if it's not on a model, I'm inclined to simplify the brake rigging on a fitted wagon for instance. Not to the extent of omitting the cross-shaft, or some semblance of the yokes between the shoes on clasp-braked wagons, but I stop short of tying them all together. I also try to make sure that dropping the lever would actually apply the brakes rather than lift them off, something which has not always been appreciated by all kit manufacturers, it seems. But if handbuilt brake gear complete with every bolt, pin, link and lever is to your taste, I fear you may be disappointed.

For couplings I always fit scale three-link or screw ones, using mainly Roxey, Maygib or PC etchings; say what you like, they look better than the automatic variety, although they can be mightily frustrating, especially at arm's length in poor light. Scale couplings really deserve sprung buffers, I suppose, but I don't use these for goods stock as a rule, at least not with short wheelbase vehicles. Buffers are a slightly difficult area, in fact: over the years some of those included in kits have been pretty dire, and although most of the common ones are available as separate white metal castings, they aren't all. So sometimes it's a case of make do or adapt.

If buffers are sometimes a compromise, however, compensation is almost a closed book to me. I have always worked in EM and compensation is frankly unnecessary in anything other than P4/S4/18.83 : if you can't make them stay on the track with overscale flanges, compensation is unlikely to help. Some people don't even compensate goods stock in S4, preferring a bit of slop in the axleboxes. Smoothly-laid pointwork, parallel, free-running axles, and a bit of added ballast in the lightest vehicles are far more important in achieving the illusion of weight and momentum. However, it would be a serious omission in a book of this kind to ignore the subject of compensation entirely in view of the growing number of modellers for whom it is indispensable. It might be thought presumptuous of someone with no real experience of the subject to try to tell others how to do it, for while I can put together a 30-wagon train of uncompensated vehicles and be reasonably assured of propelling it successfully first time through EM point and crossing work, I can't say the same for compensated stock simply because I've never done it. But I have conducted some experiments with compensation on a few of the vehicles built while this book has been in preparation, and have reached a few empirical conclusions. I can't make any claim to authority on the subject, but the ones I've built in this form do run, so I must have done something right.

Fortunately, the gods have smiled upon me in my hour of need, and Chris Pendlenton has very kindly agreed to deal with the subject of compensation in Volume 2, which rounds out to my satisfaction, and I hope to yours, what would otherwise have been a rather unbalanced treatment of the whole subject of wagon construction.

CHAPTER ONE
FIRST PRINCIPLES

It seems reasonable to start off with a brief review of the types of materials involved in building wagons, together with some of the techniques employed and tools which will be useful.

Broadly there are three materials you will come across in kits, white metal castings, injection moulded plastic and etched metal, usually brass, or various combinations of these. Each requires a different approach and different skills, and each has its advantages and disadvantages. White metal castings can, at their best, give an excellent crispness of surface detail, but at the expense of overscale thickness of fine components and considerable weight; a long trainload of white metal wagons takes a bit of shifting. The same commendable quality of detail is also achievable with moulded plastic, and plastic has the advantage of being light (sometimes too light), easy to work and easy to modify. It shares with white metal, however, a lack of strength which can only be overcome by increasing the thickness of delicate parts. Sheet metal clearly scores in terms of strength, but requires a lot more work to achieve a level of detail comparable with white metal and plastic. In fact, etched kit construction is much closer to scratchbuilding than either of the other two options, with a consequent time penalty, and this, coupled with the greater initial cost, is probably why etched brass wagon kits (as opposed to loco and coach kits) are fairly thin on the ground. By comparison, one of the chief advantages of scratchbuilding is that it allows you, within reason, to choose the best materials for each aspect of the job. For example, styrene sheet for body parts, cast metal for buffers, springs and axleboxes, and sheet metal for axleguards, V-hangers, brake levers and so on.

For white metal kits a commonly recommended method of assembly is low-melt solder. Certainly this has clear advantages over ordinary solder, but personally I have reservations over the use of anything quite so permanent as solder where it can possibly be avoided. To begin with, soldering is a job that generally needs fifteen hands to wield the iron and hold everything together at the same time, with the constantly attendant risk of singed flesh into the bargain. Paste flux is messy, and liquid flux produces fumes that burn the skin off the back of your throat.

All this may be part of the fun, but the main problem is that, however many dry runs you have, it's very difficult to get it right first time, every time, and that much harder to put right when you get it wrong – and you will, sooner or later. Take a simple job like soldering a wagon side and end together: holding them square with two hands is hard enough, never mind one, especially in cases where the inclusion of cast lugs to give a positive location is impossible because they would be visible on the finished model. A simple jig arrangement using blocks of wood glued or screwed to a portable base to give inside and outside right-angles can be very useful, especially with the help of some Blu-tack, and it's always advisable when joining major components together to solder them here and there in the first place to make sure they fit properly.

Even so, my own particular heresy is a preference for using glue for white metal – and not superglue, which is also a trifle too permanent for my taste. That is to say, that both solder and cyanacrylates suffer from immediate permanence; you can't adjust the joint while the bond hardens, as you can with five-minute epoxy, or pull the pieces apart and reglue them as you can with, say, Evostik. Solder also tends to flow beyond the joint into areas where you don't want it, and when it does so is harder to clean up than epoxy, which yields to a sharp knife. On the other hand, nothing beats solder for strength, and for vulnerable metal parts such as brake gear, or moving or stressed components, sound joints are clearly the objective. Solder is also much to be preferred for etched kit construction, of course.

With plastic the choice is more straightforward. Liquid solvent is far and away the easiest and cleanest adhesive for both moulded plastic kits and styrene sheet; the only point to watch is that some brands are more active than others. This is not necessarily an advantage unless you are working with materials that cannot easily be welded with a milder solvent, such as Mekpak, because the more active formulations (Daywat and Polyweld, for instance) have a greater capacity to attack, and therefore soften and mark plain styrene and the plastics normally used for moulded kit manufacture. Provided you're reasonably sparing with the stuff, any solvent will do the trick, of course, but I would certainly recommend a milder one for clear styrene, which stronger solvents will damage at a touch, and for applications where you need to flood a joint, such as when laminating two thicknesses of material together. I have a suspicion that the wrong choice of solvent is behind many of the horror stories of buildings warping, box vans collapsing, and surfaces softening and crinkling weeks after they should have safely stabilised. And you don't actually need anything very active for our purposes in any case.

The question also arises as to how you stick different materials to each other: plastic to white metal, for instance. Apart from paper, which can be glued to the surface of styrene with solvent (some people represent canvas-covered van roofs in this way), there's no real alternative to epoxy or an impact adhesive. Because impact adhesives are also plastic solvents, they need to be used sparingly, but for the same reason, perhaps, seem to make a stronger bond in a plain joint between two flat surfaces. Epoxy is tidier to use, however, (it doesn't string like Evostik, for instance), and can be used as a filler, and as a cement to pack round invisible joints, such as white metal or brass embellishments to a plastic underframe. Nevertheless, when fitting small components I

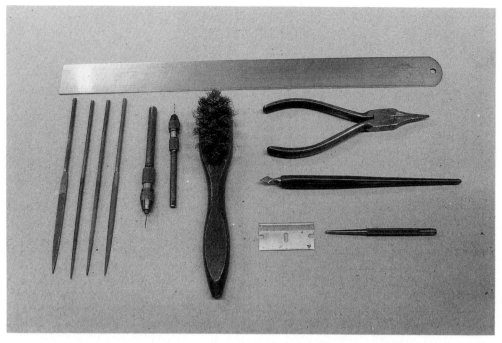

Tools of the trade.

like to give the glue a bit of help wherever possible by developing the joints into something rather more positive than plain surface-to-surface ones.

In other words it's all a matter of horses for courses, and you need to be familiar with all these materials and adhesives if you're going to exploit the full range of kits, and modifications of kits, open to you.

TOOLS

The choice of tools tends to be a rather personal thing, and over the years we all develop ways of doing things according to the tools available to us. Still, these are what I've found to be more-or-less indispensable, and at the same time sufficient to handle all the materials you're likely to have to deal with.

A good steel rule is essential, preferably a foot long and marked in both imperial and metric measurements down to $\frac{1}{64}$ inch and 0.5 mm. Apart from scaling distances, obvious uses include scribing and cutting plastic sheet, checking for distortions in supposedly straight edges and flat surfaces, and not least as a set-square – something I've never had.

Equally important is a good pair of small pliers, the smaller the better, and preferably with plain, not serrated, jaws. Rather than conventional needle-nosed pliers with rounded backs, I use a pair of circlip pliers which have squared jaws tapering to a very fine point; each jaw is less than a millimetre square at the tip –

indispensable for bending metal and plastic rod and strip, holding small parts for filing or soldering, and even locating components in places your fingers won't reach. For some jobs, however, like bending up larger etched parts, a bigger pair of pliers is useful, and these should be square across the end.

A set of small files will be needed whatever materials you're working with. Although it's not essential to vary the coarseness, a finer cut is more suitable for metal, especially sheet metal, and a rougher cut for plastic. White metal and plastic will quite quickly clog a file, and a wire suede brush is useful for cleaning, but may not shift white metal filings which I generally resort to picking out with a needle in a pin chuck.

That's something else you'll need, together with a selection of drill bits. Most useful in my experience are $\frac{1}{64}$ inch, 0.45 mm (for 26 swg wire), 0.52 mm (for 20-thou plastic rod), $\frac{1}{32}$ inch (for 30-thou rod), 2 mm (for axle bearings, although a slightly smaller one will give a nice push fit in plastic), and a larger one, say about $\frac{1}{8}$ inch, for countersinking. Intermediate sizes can be obtained by working a smaller bit in and out in the chuck, or, if they're larger than $\frac{1}{32}$ inch, by reaming with a round file. A small hand drill is also useful when drilling sheet metal, which takes for ever with a pin chuck; it tends to be more destructive of small bits, though. A centre punch will be necessary to locate the drill in sheet metal, but has other uses as well:

as a drift to press home axle bearings, for instance, or as a makeshift riveting tool, again for sheet metal.

For cutting plastic, most people use a craft knife or scalpel, which is fine. My own preference is for what used to be called single-edged razor blades: ordinary razor blades are no use because they're not rigid enough, even in a holder, but single-edged ones are thicker with a spine along one edge, which allows you to put a lot of pressure right on the point when you need to, without the risk of the blade cockling sideways. Unfortunately, they're rather hard to get nowadays, but they are occasionally sold in small packs in supermarkets and the like as craft knives. When it comed to metal, a decent pair of scissors takes a lot of beating, but you might get less distortion with a pair of proper shears, and a piercing saw is needed for thicker material.

Another cutting tool I wouldn't be without, although I don't use it much for that purpose, is a scraperboard knife. These are available from art shops and come with a variety of blade shapes, though a simple vee serves my purpose. I use it for scribing lines in plastic sheet: held upright against a straightedge like a pencil with the point on the work surface and the blade at right-angles to the line, with the flat side facing in the direction of movement, the point will gouge a clean furrow in the material, the depth varying according to how hard you press as you draw it along. Most of the swarf comes away at the time, and a quick pass with a file across the surface, followed by a scrub with a wire suede brush will remove the rest. The knife edges proper are on both sides of the vee (a good reason for having a *steel* straightedge), and can be used instead of a file to scrape burrs and sharp edges off exposed corners. It is also strong enough to use for scraping or paring away excess solder.

Speaking of which, you can't do without a soldering iron, preferably one that takes different bit sizes, and minimum 15-watt. Keep the bit(s) tinned and clean (another use for the suede brush) and file it down and re-tin if it shows signs of pitting. One of the causes of pitting is said to be carrying solder on the bit, rather than bringing the iron and the solder together to the workpiece, but it comes down to how many hands you've got, and it's almost impossible to avoid most of the time. Even with only one hand for the iron, an extra two or three to hold everything together wouldn't go amiss. Unfortunately, vices and pliers tend to act as heat sinks, and fingers burn easily, so when soldering small parts together I find a block of balsa quite useful. The wood is soft enough to push a piece of strip or wire into it at almost any angle, but will then hold it firmly while you adjust the second part with one hand and solder with the other. Wherever possible, leave a stalk on the thing you're holding so that your fingers don't form the heat sink. Occasionally, it might be difficult to cut this stalk off afterwards; if it looks as if it could be inaccessible, file it partly through so that it will snap off at about the right point when you're ready.

GENERAL PRINCIPLES

It's not my intention at this point to embark on a detailed description of wagon-building, but a few general principles might be useful before we get down to looking at individual wagons. Hopefully most of the finer points will crop up somewhere along the line in relation to specific vehicles; so, for instance, if you're dying to know about making brake/hand wheels, you'll have to wait until I get to the first vehicle that has them (bulk grain vans, as it happens).

Before beginning any project I like to assemble as much data on the vehicle in question as I can. Much of this comes from published sources, sometimes from my own photographs, most of which, however, have been taken in the last ten years and show wagons in the later stages

Use of the scraperboard knife.

of life, often altered from their original form. Information quoted in the instructions accompanying a kit should not always be taken at face value, I'm afraid; sample numbers, in particular, too often relate to wagons with significant detail differences. So I prefer to find a picture of a vehicle as running at about the period I'm modelling, and to incorporate any detail variations that are visible. This can't be a hard and fast rule, I have to admit; wagons have never been the favourite subject of most railway photographers, and the further back you go, the harder it gets. But it's comforting to know whenever possible that the wagon you're building actually ran in the condition portrayed.

Before separating any parts from the sprue or etched sheet they're attached to, try to visualise how they're going to fit together. Don't be in a hurry to make the first incision in case you remove a vital bit. If in doubt, err on the safe side, and if all else fails, read the instructions. They will generally tell you to start with the body, and if so leave the underframe parts unseparated for the time being; they're easier to find that way. Whatever material the kit is made of, but especially if it's plastic or white metal, you will almost certainly have some cleaning up to do to remove flash, pips and moulding lines, and generally to prepare edges and surfaces that will remain visible or mate with others. Poor joints are often a result of

failing to file mating surfaces flat, and the best ones are those that make the most of the potential surface area. Rebated joints are the strongest, where one of the components has a recess built into it for the other one to sit in; they also make for very precise location of the parts. Butt joints are not quite so strong and are more difficult to disguise satisfactorily, but they are still preferable in many ways to a bad mitred joint. On the face of it, mitres have a lot going for them, a relatively large surface area and a fairly inconspicuous joint line right on the angle of the corner – especially if you file a slight radius on it to remove the unprototypical knife-edge. But this is only true of an absolutely perfect mitre. Too often the surfaces are not smooth, or worse, not cut at the same angle, and they only join where they touch. Careful preparation is essential to make the most of mitred joints in terms of both their effectiveness and their appearance.

For the scratch-builder especially, another problem with joints, and particularly mitred ones, I feel, is the common tendency for the sides to bow inwards after construction. Certainly my experience is that avoiding mitred corners tends to reduce the effect significantly, and that the phenomenon has far more to do with this cause then it has with either the thickness of the material used or whether or not the planking is scribed on both sides – which of course it should be. But there is a foolproof solution in any case: bow the sides outwards first. There were few wooden-bodied open wagons of four planks or more that didn't acquire a characteristic bulge after a period in service, and if you bend the sides in your fingers before assembly, the worst that is likely to happen is that they will then pull straight again. Vans seem less prone to the infection than open wagons, but they can usually be braced internally if you feel there is a real risk of it happening.

Whatever the instructions may say, I prefer to put together the sides and ends first without the floor. It's far easier to get clean, tidy corner joints this way, because too often the floor is not exactly the right size, and if it needs trimming or extending, this should be done evenly on all offending edges, at least wherever the underside of the floor incorporates lugs or pips to locate underframe components. Even adjustment is impossible once you've stuck any of the sides or ends in place. So I make it a rule to attach each pair of sides and ends together first, and then to stick the two assemblies to each other, before inserting the floor. This does make it slightly more difficult to ensure that each corner is a true right-angle, but you can use the floor as a template, or a set-square, to help you judge the accuracy of each corner. In any case, provided you're using glue or a solvent, and don't separate the insertion of the floor from the assembly of the sides and ends by more than an hour or so, there will be enough give in the joints for the body to adjust itself to the floor when you come to slot it in.

I've concentrated on this early part of the assembly because it's vital to make certain at this stage that the model is as square in all planes as it possibly can be. Both appearance and true running depend upon it. Don't be satisfied, therefore, just to get the corners clean and right-angled; make sure that the tops of the sides match exactly with the ends, and that the undersides of the headstocks are parallel in both planes. If they're not, find out why, and correct it. A bit of time and trouble now will pay dividends later. It may be that, despite your care, one of the corners is not quite square in all respects, perhaps because the mating surfaces or interlocking joints haven't been cleaned up properly. It may be that the parts are twisted, or irregular in some way. Whatever the reason, it's better to put it right now than to have to make adjustments to the running gear in order to get the wagon to sit on all four wheels.

The first element of the running gear to consider is bearings. Pin-point axles and turned brass bearings have been around long enough now to make them accepted as the standard system in all kit and scratch-building applications where outside axleboxes are involved. However, although the axle length over the pin-points has been established as 26 mm, getting the bearings exactly the right distance apart is not always as simple as it ought to be. The principle is clear enough: clear the hole in the axlebox to the correct depth with a 2 mm/No. 47 drill so that the lip or flange on the bearings sits snugly against the back of the axleguard, and the bearings will automatically be properly spaced to accept the axles with minimal end float. Well, sometimes they are, but mostly they're not, and it's certainly asking for trouble to assemble a kit that you're not familiar with in the blithe assumption that the wheelsets will fit properly first time.

You need to check *before* you stick the critical parts together that the axles won't be trapped too tightly or left too slack. How you check this, and how you put any faults right, will depend to some extent on the design of the kit. Where the solebars and axleguards are integral with the body sides, don't go beyond the first stage of body construction – sticking each pair of sides and ends together – without inserting the bearings and then bringing the two halves together with the wheelsets in place. If you do this with the body upside-down on a level surface (easy with an open wagon, rather less so with a van), you can establish whether the two corner joints will mate properly. If not, the bearings need widening out, either by countersinking the holes they sit in with a drill bit slightly larger than the circumference of the flange on the bearing, or by the use of flangeless bearings (which I don't like very much, because once you've put them in they're little devils to get out again). If the corners are okay, see how much end float ('slop') there is in the axles. Excessive slop can be cured by inserting a plastic collar behind the bearing flange: drill a 2 mm hole in a piece of styrene sheet of the right thickness (that is, about half of the amount of slop you want to take out), and chop round it about a millimetre clear of the hole. Repeat for the other side, slot the bearings into them, and refit. Some adjustment is also possible by careful selection of bearings (not all are turned to the same depth, and I like to keep a stock acquired from various sources), and by slightly bending cast axleguards – but beware unsightly splayed W-irons.

These same methods of adjustment can also be used for kits which have separate solebars and for axleguards. With these kits, of course, you can assemble the body completely first, and it should then be possible to locate the solebars with bearings fitted and wheelsets in place accurately enough to check the spacing without gluing them in. Now you have the extra option of adjusting the position of the solebars by putting plastic shims between them and whatever locating lugs there may be, or by filing down the backs of the solebars, depending on whether you need to push them out or pull them in. Bear in mind, however, that after 1923 the prototypical distance across the faces of the solebars was 6 ft 3 ins., plus the thickness of the material, generally five inches on each side for wooden-framed wagons, and something less than half-an-inch for steel ones. So mucking about with the spacing of the solebars is not something that can be done without regard to the accurate appearance of the wagon – assuming, of course, that the solebars were correctly-spaced to start with, and that compromises had not already been made to allow for the often overscale thickness of the materials used in the kit.

If the solebars can't be located firmly enough to check the spacing reliably, it will be necessary to glue one into position first, which rather restricts the scope for altering the other one, and brings you back to adjusting the bearings. Similarly with separate axleguards, which in any case don't really lend themselves to major adjustment, although it's usually possible to set them in a bit by inserting packing against the backs of the solebars. Whatever the design of the kit, however, don't be in a hurry to glue the bearings in place, because you may need to take them out again before you've finished. In fact, you don't really need to glue them in at all; even if they seem rather loose, the axles will hold them in and the wagon will run quite happily in this condition.

Without doubt the most reliable spacing is achieved with the use of etched axleguards. Even here, there is some scope for varying the distance between the bearings according to exactly where you make the folds, and the depth of the cone in the bearings will also play a part. Fortunately, as with white metal, you can bend the axleguards in or out a bit without it being too noticeable, and you will generally find that the gap between the axleguards will work out at about 24 mm., plus or minus 10 thou. Another useful dimension that helps to fix the amount of packing you need between the unit and the floor, is that the distance from the underside of the solebar to the centre of the bearing scales out at $5\frac{1}{2}$ to 6 mm (it varies slightly from wagon to wagon). An important point to watch when folding up the units is to make each fold at right-angles to the axis between the bearing holes; otherwise you risk mounting the unit with the axles askew.

Getting the wheels to revolve freely between properly-spaced axleguards is only half the battle. At the same time as you're making them run smoothly, you must be checking to make sure that the wagon will sit upright with all four wheels on the rails (we're talking rigid under-frames here, you understand). Even this is not the end of the story; the axles must also be parallel to each other when viewed from underneath, *and* at right-angles to the longitudinal axis of the wagon. Uncertain progress through pointwork, jarring contact of flanges with crossing vees and check rails, and, at worst, derailments, can all arise because either the axles, or the flanges, or both, are out of line with each other.

The use of a sheet of plate glass has long been recommended as an infallible method of getting all the wheels on the ground at the same time. I have reservations about this: as with the bearings, you need to make sure that the wagon won't rock *before* you stick the critical parts together, and trying to hold everything in place with the precision necessary to check that the flanges all touch the floor is at best an unreliable business and at worst well nigh impossible. Rather than trying to stand the wagon on its wheels, therefore, hold the vehicle upside-down, and at the same time as you are setting the gaps between the axleguards and bearings, view the axles from the wagon end at eye level against a light surface. This will give you a perfectly reliable check as to whether they are parallel or not; if they are, the wagon won't rock and there's no more to be said. If they're not, you may need to do something about it.

This photograph of a Ratio GWR iron mink is included to show how not *to assemble a kit: the axles are way out of parallel, as indeed are the headstocks. Routine precautions will enable disasters like this to be avoided.*

I say 'may' because using pin-point axles does allow you to leave enough end float for the axles to find their own level, since the coned ends of the axles will slide in and out of the bearings, altering the horizontal attitude of the axles in the process, and making them free to compensate for minor track irregularities. Provided it's not overdone, an element of slop is acceptable, and can even be substituted for full compensation. Too much is unhealthy, however, and can result in unpredictable behaviour of the wagon, especially when being propelled round bends and through pointwork. In building rigid underframes, anything more than minimal end float smacks to me of poor workmanship, and I try to avoid it.

So if I find that a pair of axles aren't parallel when viewed at eye level, I try to put it right. If the solebars and axleguards are integral with the body sides, this may just be a matter of minor misalignment at a corner joint, but if the body is otherwise square it would be wise not to tamper with it at this stage. If the solebars are separate, the easiest thing to do is either to file a few thou off the top edge of one of them at one end, or to insert a sliver of 5 or 10-thou plastic between the solebar and the floor at the diagonally opposite corner. Which you choose will depend to some extent on whether raising or lowering one corner will have any noticeable effect on how the wagon sits on the track; whilst lop-sided or end-heavy vehicles were by no means unknown, I'm assuming that we don't want to build in such aberrations by accident. An alternative route to try, and the only one to follow if the solebars and sides are integral, is to enlarge the hole in the back of the axlebox either upwards or downwards by working a 2 mm drill bit around in your fingers, putting a modicum of pressure in the direction you want to go. This is a bit rough-and-ready, but it works, provided you don't widen the hole in other directions in the process. When you've taken out enough material to re-locate the bearing as required, slip a bit of thin plastic into the hole on the other side to wedge the bearing in its new position, and if it seems at all insecure, fix it with a dab of epoxy.

This process is a lot easier if you're using etched axleguards, of course. To begin

EM Gauge Society etched BR axleguards (note the distinctive horse/capstan hook holes). On the left, a pair of axleguards as bought, together with a cradle unit. In the centre, one of each has been bent up ready to be fitted together, and on the right is another set hinged with a length of wire. Make sure that there is just enough free movement to enable the unit to rock freely without sliding up and down on the hinge pin, and that the holes are a bare clearance fit so that there is no turning movement to take the axle out of square to the axis of the body.

Fig. 1 Brake lever arrangements

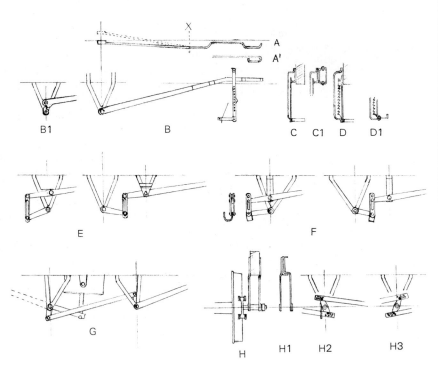

A   Profile of Standard RCH brake lever for independent brakegear with double V-hangers. Profile for single V-hanger shown dotted. Offset from face of wooden solebar at point X is 3 5/8 inches.

A1   Alternative handle.

B   Relationship of V-hanger, lever and lever guard. Lever tapers evenly from 4 inches wide at pivot to 2 inches at handle. Lever guard generally 2 inches wide.

B1   Morton clutch arrangement, usually on same side as brakes when these are fitted to one side only.

C   Lever guard and stay bracket: wooden solebar.

C1   Scrap view of method of attachment to steel solebar.

D   GW style of toothed rack. Rack is on left-hand side when viewed from front.

D1   Alternative style of stay bracket.

E   BR slotted link brakegear (both sides shown). Right-hand side layout also used for some LNER vehicles, e.g. grain hoppers, 20 ton loco coal wagons (opposite side as B). Bottom lever may fit either side of V-hanger, and is cranked more or less accordingly.

F   One style of SR fitted brakegear (both sides shown). Note shape of connection between slotted link and bottom lever. Vertical bracket cranked outwards below solebar.

G   LNER fitted brakegear. Opposite side has single V-hanger in position, denoted by dotted lever; these two V-hangers linked by cross-shaft, on which inclined vacuum cylinder acts. Vac. cylinder on side with single V-hanger.

H   Section through independent brake gear. Note joggle in V-hangers required in 1923 RCH specification. Note also offset of wheels in relation to inner ends of push rods, requiring rods to be angled in a shallow vee. However, if cross shaft fitted, tumbler is mounted in line with wheels.

H1   Alternative V-hanger layout with steel solebars.

H2   Arrangement of tumbler and push rods: direct-acting lever.

H3   Reversed layout on Morton clutch side.

NOTE: Detailed dimensions and layouts vary tremendously. These sketches illustrate a selection of patterns at an approximate scale of 1½ times full size for 4mm, but should be taken as no more than a guide to certain types of linkage employed.

with, there is often enough movement of the bearing in the hole in the axleguard to permit fine adjustment, but if there isn't, it's a simple matter to unsolder the bearing, enlarge the hole a little with a round file in the desired direction, and then hold the bearing in its new position with a needle while you solder it in again. My block of balsa has a bearing-sized hole drilled in it to enable the axleguard to lie flat so that the bearing can be held securely when soldering – the only time that I automatically fix the bearings in position is when using etched axleguards.

The other potential misalignment problem you need to watch out for is ending up with the axles out of square to the fore-and-aft axis of the wagon. Provided you've put the body together squarely (and if you haven't, you've just not been listening), this is usually attributable to trimming too much off the end of one solebar in order to get it to fit between the headstocks. If you need to trim the solebars in this way, make sure you do it evenly and equally on both of them, and then check with the axles in position before gluing them in. You may sometimes overdo the trimming, in which case you can restore a good interference fit by wedging a sliver of plastic between solebar and headstock.

Alternatively, you may find that you've got only one of the axles out of square. This is mainly a problem that afflicts the scratchbuilder, and I'm annoyed when I do it because it's really pure carelessness. But it can also affect compensated wagons, either because the rocking unit has been fitted out of true, or because there is enough play in the unit to enable it to turn as well as rock. This is one inherent disadvantage of the tab-and-slot method of mounting. And lastly, it can also crop up with those kits which have separate axleguards, where the location of each one on the solebar may not be too precise. The answer is to take care not to let it happen in the first place, but if you do find that you have to correct it after assembly, the only remedy is to enlarge the axle bearing hole as previously described, but laterally rather than vertically.

Having assembled the body, underframe and running gear so that the wagon performs faultlessly (God willing), we now need to add the bits and pieces to make sure it looks as good as it runs. Each of these will be dealt with in some detail in looking at individual wagons, but a few general points may not go amiss at this stage.

In common with all the manufacturers of ready-to-run equipment, who generally, I'm afraid, offer us underframes of a much lower standard than the bodies above them, there is a tendency among most kit makers to pay less attention to what goes on below the body. However impressive the upperworks may be, underframe detail takes a back seat, and nowhere is this more apparent than on the subject of brakes. Too often these are ill-fitting, coarse and poorly-detailed, and were it not for a number of small parts suppliers dealing in cast and etched components, I would have to say that things in this area had barely improved in twenty years or more. I'm the first to admit that fully-detailed brake rigging is beyond my own aspirations, but such basic omissions as cross-shafts and vacuum pipes really should be a thing of the past.

Happily, as I hope to show, a lot is achievable with a bit of effort. For example, one area where kits haven't moved with the times is in the matter of brake levers and guards. White metal and plastic are not ideal materials for these, and there are some pretty weird and wonderful shapes out there masquerading as the real thing and capable of only limited improvement. There is no real substitute for brass or nickel-silver strip, and if you can't locate suitable etchings (and these aren't widely advertised), making your own is not especially difficult. There are only two main parts to each one, the lever and guard each being made in one piece. The lever consists of a tapering piece of strip roughly cut from a sheet of 10 to 15-thou thickness, and then filed to shape. The accompanying diagram gives an idea of the shape and dimensions of a standard RCH pattern lever, and although variations were common, most of the features were recognisably present in other types. If the design and layout of the brake gear lends itself to attaching the bottom end of the lever to a cross-shaft, drill a $\frac{1}{32}$ inch hole at the fulcrum.

The diagram also shows how to bend to shape a length of strip of not more than 10-thou thickness, about 30 mm long and three-quarters of a millimetre wide, to make the guard. If you wish you can drill the pin holes and include the lug at the side for the pin and chain; I never have, but I do like to incorporate a spigot at the top of the guard which can be force-fitted

Fig. 2 One-piece lever guard.

Spigot through solebar

Solder here to locate lever and hold guard together

Stay bracket

A pair of brake levers and guards made up as described in this chapter. Note the spigot for attaching the unit to the solebar, and the bracing strap at the foot of the guard; this will be bent to shape and trimmed on final assembly.

through a hole in the solebar, and a stay to attach the foot to the nearest axleguard—brake levers are too often only held on by a wing and a prayer. You don't need to solder the lever and guard together, but it makes a stronger job, and if you do, it should be done before fitting. I hold the base of the lever in a hand vice, using a free finger and thumb to locate the guard; a quick touch with the iron, and hopefully the finished product is reasonably square. An alternative would be to jam the lever or the guard into the all-purpose block of balsa while the deed is done. Similarly the bottom stay is held in the balsa while soldering, and only bent and trimmed to length when the unit is finally ready to be fitted to the wagon.

With the brakes themselves, I've always felt that it's important to get the shoes in line with the wheels and as close to the tyres as possible – even with the brakes off, the shoes on the real things are still more-or-less rubbing the tyres. We don't want them to bind on the model, of course, so some clearance is essential, and you may need to chamfer the backs of the shoes; but I've come across kits where the brake moulding needs to be lengthened by

A slightly posed photograph demonstrating why the hand brake lever was shaped as it was to clear the axlebox. Full marks for the polished boots, but shouldn't he really be using a brake stick? The wagon appears to be of pre-grouping origin from one of the LNER's constituents. The chamfered top edge of the body side planks was a normal feature of wooden body construction.

Although the vehicle shown on these pages is a tank wagon built after nationalization, this style of independent brakegear with double vee-hangers was applied to many kinds of wagon over a long period, and could be fitted to both wooden- and steel-framed vehicles.

up to 2 mm just to get the shoes within spitting distance of the wheels. Just as brake levers can be fairly representational, the same goes for the various components of the brake assembly, especially the shoes themselves. Just how far you go in replacing these is up to you, but you'll find a few ideas if you read on.

An important key to a successful model, I believe, is an understanding of how the brakes work. This will help to save you from pitfalls by explaining why they were as they were, and which bit did what; it's always useful I think, whatever you're modelling, to know the mechanics of something, since this helps you to interpret drawings and photographs, and to reproduce them more accurately. There were far too many different designs to describe them all here, but most of the major reference books include good information, and for an in-depth study of the basic RCH independent style you can do no better than read Chris Croft's articles in *MRJs* 12–15. For now, just remember that if the two brake levers are linked by a cross shaft, there must be some mechanism for the action of one to be reversed, either by a cam or clutch, or by additional linkage of some sort. In this case, if there are brakes on both sides, the two mouldings must not be be identical, because each pair of upper pushrods acts on one wheelset, and each pair of lower ones on the other. Only with independent either-side brakes with two V-hangers on each side can both sets of brakegear be the same.

Another problem that affects plastic kits in particular is the relative weakness of some of the parts on and below the solebar. I've mentioned the susceptibility of brake levers, which are both fairly delicate and lightly attached, and the same can be true of door springs, axleguard tie bars and vacuum pipes. You will see that in many cases I replace these in metal, because the experience of operating exhibition layouts has shown that they are very vulnerable to damage or falling off in use. Plastic buffers, too, can suffer breakages, although I generally replace these with white metal ones only when the appearance of the plastic buffers is sub-standard in any way, or when modelling a wagon fitted with a different pattern. In this connection it may be useful to point out that wagons with continuous brakes usually had longer buffers than unfitted ones, and this includes vehicles converted to vacuum in later life; one rather makeshift method of doing this was to weld a $2\frac{1}{2}$ inch collar onto the end

of the buffer guide to extend the overall length from 18 to $20\frac{1}{2}$ inches.

For the record, the standard spacing of buffers on the headstock should be 5 ft 8 ins, give or take half an inch – 22.5 to just under 23 mm. It's important to check with any kit that this dimension is accurate, and, if it isn't, to correct it if possible. Up to a millimetre out either way is not unknown, and discrepancies such as this are a recipe for buffer-locking when propelling, especially if the amount of end float in the axles allows one or both wagons an excessive degree of side-throw as well. And if one of them is also particularly light, the chances of misbehaviour are increased still further. I have no magic formula to offer in the matter of weight, and frankly I doubt if it's as critical as all that, but all-plastic kits are less inclined to part company with the rails when a bit of ballast is added. As a rule of thumb, unless you've included a number of cast metal components, and more than just buffers, springs and axleboxes, stick some scrap white metal or lead sheet, about enough to double the wagon's original weight, under the floor.

The subject of vacuum pipes on fitted vehicles is a slightly contentious one: it's impracticable in the smaller scales to model vac. pipes that can be connected and disconnected like the real thing, so much of the time the pipe will be in the wrong position. But leaving them off looks even worse. When not in use they were supposed to be clipped back onto the dumb connection on the wagon end, but in practice they seem to have been left dangling more often than not, so this is how I model them. I don't normally use

commercial products, which I've found are mostly deficient in either appearance or security of fitting, although I suppose I'm sticking my neck out to criticize the appearance of others when my own are just bent up from thick paper-clip wire. But at least the *shape* reminds me of the real thing, and they have the other distinct advantage of great strength, especially if you bend the tail up behind the headstock so that it clips firmly in place and can be cemented with a blob of epoxy – though even this is wrong, of course, since the pipe usually ran the length of the wagon below the level of the underframe.

Bearing in mind everything I've said so far, people may be surprised that not all the wagons described here are embellished to exactly the same level in all departments: that with one I replace cast or moulded brake levers with sheet metal ones, for example, but with another make do with what is offered in the kit, and even use parts that I've criticized or replaced elsewhere. My only excuse is that I'm setting out to show where improvements are possible, and how to go about them. In effect, I'm describing a series of options, and I'm not trying to suggest that any kit will be ruined if you don't take them, or choose to go another way. No single wagon will illustrate the whole picture, but I hope that by the end of this survey most parts of the jigsaw will have been fitted into place, and that each of the wagons we shall be looking at will make a contribution to the whole by describing various aspects of prototype design and alternative techniques of reproducing it in miniature.

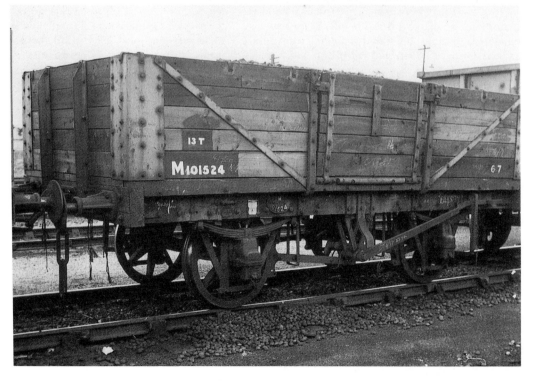

A quartet of well-nigh identical wagons to LMS Diagram 1666. All were photographed in BR days towards the end of their lives and are generally down-at-heel, although M156572 seems to have kept most of its light grey paintwork. Originally designed for a 12-ton load, all have been uprated to 13 tons in common with many other types during World War 2. Three of the four seem to have no rope cleats of any sort, resulting in the wagon sheet on M266588 being secured to sundry other projections around solebar level. The load of coal in M156572 was a practice officially frowned upon, I believe, but common enough all the same.
ROYE ENGLAND

CHAPTER TWO
OPEN WAGONS

LMS OPEN

The ubiquitous high-sided open merchandise wagon was one of the most common types in steam days, and bidding fair to be the most common among them was Diagram 1666 of the LMSR, almost 55,000 of which were built to a design of Midland origin over the first eight years from the Grouping. Minor variations crept in during this period (position of label clips and wagon plates, angle of cutaway on end stanchions, shape of spring saddle above the axleboxes, etc), but, broadly-speaking, ABS's cast metal kit can be used to model any and all of them. Numbering was random, but nine different ones are quoted in the instructions, and if that's not enough for you, there are another thirty in *An Illustrated History of LMS Wagons*, together with numerous photographs.

With sides, solebars and axleguards in one piece, this must rank as one of the most straightforward types of wagon kit

around, but some time and effort are still needed to make the most of it. The first job is to clean up each of the castings. A certain amount of flash was evident on the mitred corners and on the rear face of the buffer heads, and the recess in the solebar for the combined V-hanger and door spring casting was more or less filled up at the top. The tops of the sides had a row of pips which needed filing down, and too-obvious mould lines had to be removed from the ends of the headstocks and the outer face of the buffer heads; for the same reason, the buffer bases had to be tidied up by thinning down the rear face at one side so that they could be mounted square to the headstocks. Then, having chosen to model M234421 in more or less the condition shown in *An Illustrated History of LMS Wagons*, I removed the rope cleats from below the body sides and filed the faces of the spring saddles flush and the tops level. Finally, because I was going to fit three-link couplings, I removed the cast pegs for the tension-lock

type by scoring with a blade and snapping them off with a pair of pliers.

At this stage, you might also consider replacing the cast door springs, which are exceedingly thick and rather awkward to thin down without damaging the V-hanger which surrounds each one. In fact I didn't on this occasion, although I did alter the identical fitting on ABS's LMS mineral wagon. A number of methods suggest themselves, all involving the use of brass or nickel-silver strip; you could remove the whole of the casting both on and below the solebar and replace it with a new one soldered to the face of the solebar, impressing the fixing bolts from the rear first with a centre-punch (or a riveting tool if you run to one). Or you could just cut off the projecting part below the solebar, and bend the new one so that it clips round the rear of the solebar, which is perhaps preferable if you're assembling with glue; the epoxy will help to hide the joint between the metal strip and the remaining cast part above it, and it avoids

the need to glue two flat, plain surfaces together, which can result in a suspect joint when attaching small components. A third possibility involving a bit more work would be to remove the whole spring as first described, but to reproduce the bolt heads by soldering lengths of wire into holes in the new spring and then drilling corresponding holes in the solebar, giving a more positive joint which would be suitable for either solder or glue. Yet another option, is to solder two bits of strip together, leave one straight to fit on the face of the solebar, and bend the other to clip round the back; bearing in mind that the real thing consisted of two pieces of metal, this is possibly the most realistic in appearance.

Whichever road you choose to take, however, don't be in too much of a hurry to fit the V-hanger/spring unit. Unlike the spring, the vee itself is quite delicate, and even though the inner vee is integral with the solebar, my inclination would be to assemble the main castings first, because this can involve a measure of rough hand-

Fig. 3 Side door spring fitting.

Suggested methods of attaching sheet metal springs to wood and steel solebars, avoiding simple surface-to-surface joints. Shape of springs varied considerably, but the standard width was 4 inches; reduce to fit 1/32 inch hole when slotted through solebar.

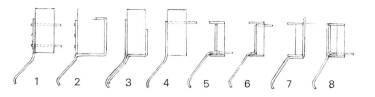

1 Uses wire for spigots and bolt detail.
2 Leaves cast detail on solebar face — ABS only.
5 Uses styrene strip for detail on solebar face.
8 Applies where spring is bracketed clear of solebar: two lengths of strip soldered together.

The lettering on this wagon presents a few puzzles. Apart from the italic style of the tare weight, and the painting of the number on a grey panel rather than a black one, it has been suggested that the markings on the side door indicate a repaired wagon re-using sections of planking from a condemned vehicle. Paintwork apart, however, this is another standard D1666 wagon.
ROYE ENGLAND

ling. To begin with, the castings may have become distorted before they reach you, and the instructions wisely advise checking for this before going any further. However, this is not the end of the story: in my case, at least, I found it necessary to twist and tweak the sides and the axleguards quite a bit during assembly to get the whole lot square and to ensure a good fit in the axles. The instructions are a trifle laconic on what is probably the most crucial part of the whole exercise. 'Assemble sides and ends together,' they say, 'with wheels in place upside-down on a flat plate. Before glue finally hardens stand on wheels to ensure vehicle sits square on track.' This begs a number of questions, in particular, do you assemble all four sides and ends in one go; if so, how do you hold it all together and ensure a good fit for the axles (i.e. not too tight or slack) at the same time; and what do you do if the vehicle refuses to sit square, bearing in mind that the glue is going off rapidly while you ponder on the injustices of the world?

What you must do is to assemble each pair of sides and ends separately first. If you're using epoxy, as I did, this means that once you're satisfied of a good mitre and have coated the mating surfaces sparingly with the mixture, you have a tedious two or three minutes holding the parts together as accurately as possible until the glue starts to harden. At this point make any adjustments, including checking that you've got a true right-angle, and then stand each unit upside-down on a flat surface to ensure that the top edges are level. Make a final check for squareness and consistent mitre, and leave until good and hard.

Once you have two pairs of sides and ends firmly attached, you can bring them together to test the mitres between them. Unless you're very lucky, this is where the twisting and tweaking comes in, but with a bit of effort two more good corners should result. Now is the time to drill out the bearing holes in the backs of the axleboxes to see how the axles fit. With the bearings in place, bring the two side/end assemblies together again upside-down on your flat surface and insert the wheelsets. All being well, you should be able to mitre the corners again without trapping the axles too tightly or leaving them too slack; a small amount of slop, say up to 0.5 mm, won't do any harm, but in this case I found that the corners wouldn't mitre at all, so I countersunk the bearing holes with an

The basic wagon kit: only four major cast parts, plus a plastic floor, complete the body and underframe for this ABS LMS high-sided open. Even brake- and buffing-gear only account for another ten pieces between them.

oversize drill bit, working it round in my fingers, and tried again, checking at the same time that the axleguards were more or less vertical. A certain amount of fine tuning is possible by bending the axleguards in or out a bit, but what you can't do with a white metal kit is to spring the axles in and out once the thing is assembled (not often, anyway), so it's important to get it right at this stage. Incidentally, if you do disturb the axleguards, make sure that you haven't inadvertently distorted the sides at the same time and destroyed the mitre.

Once you're happy with the end float, check that the axles are (a) square to the longitudinal axis of the body, and (b) parallel with each other when viewed from the end. If not, more tweaking is called for. Only when the vehicle passes all tests should you contemplate gluing the two side/end assemblies together with the wheels in place. Once again stand the wagon upside-down till the glue goes off: provided it has passed test (b), it won't be necessary to risk disturbing the corners by trying to stand it on its wheels. Fit the plastic floor as described in the instructions.

From here on, it's all downhill, and you can fit the rest of the parts in more or less any order. When fitting the buffers, make sure that the short rib is uppermost so that your 4 mm shunter can rest his pole between it and the collar on the end of the buffer guide when doing his thing. The instructions are explicit about this, but less so when it comes to the brakeshoe castings. These are reversible (a useful feature, as we shall see in due course), and it is import-

ant to ensure that they are the right way round, so that lowering the brake lever actually puts them on instead of taking them off. The units themselves clip over lugs on the rear of the solebar, and should be fitted so that when viewed the right way up, the lower push rod is on the left. Before fitting the units, however, cut away the central vertical rib between the carrier block and the top of the tumbler: the instructions are silent on it, but this rib is totally superfluous, and is presumably only there for technical or strengthening reasons. You may also wish to think about replacing the solid cast safety loops with metal strip ones: if so, they can be epoxied into holes drilled in the carrier block. Actually, I don't feel that the cast ones are all that conspicuous, and they certainly aren't as obvious as the deficiencies with the brake lever and guard castings. Even these are worlds better than the abortionate efforts that some manufacturers inflict upon us, but they are rather heavy, and, as they fell out of the packet, rather strangely shaped. In particular the sharp reverse bend in the lever that enables it to clear the axlebox when lowered is a rather gradual, lazy affair. Whilst there is no real alternative to complete replacement with a strip metal one, the casting is capable of some improvement: careful bending with pliers can crank the lever more sharply where it's supposed to be bent and straighten it where it isn't, aided by judicious filing in front of and behind the bend. You can also reduce the apparent thickness of the top edge by filing a bevel on the rear face, and simulate the shape of the handle end of the lever in the same way. Lastly, the guard itself will stand a modicum of filing to reduce its width and thickness.

A common problem with model brake levers in service is their tendency to fall, or get knocked, off, or even broken. This is partly because they are vulnerably located, (the real things were often bent and broken in service), but also because it's difficult to attach them securely. With this kit we are luckier than some, because a peg at the top of the guard locates in a slot in the solebar, but on the original the bottom end of the guard was also braced wherever possible,

usually with a metal strap to the nearest axleguard. On a model, compensation would defeat this aim, at least at one end, but with this exception it is possible to add this strap wherever the full-size wagon had it, and it adds significantly to the rigidity of the lever/guard assembly. In this case, I bent up a length of brass strip, filing down one end to form a spigot to be epoxied into a 0.5 mm hole drilled into the back of the brake guard at its foot. A tongue at the other end was glued to the axleguard as per the prototype.

One minor feature apparently shared by all vehicles to this diagram, but not reproduced on the kit, is the spring stops fitted to the underside of the solebars above each axlebox. Indeed there were very few wagons of any type that didn't have them in some form. In this case they are apparently solid castings, which I reproduced by first epoxying a short length (2 mm or thereabouts) of 5-thou plastic strip to the bottom edge of the solebar, and then adding a tiny rectangle of 20-thou strip to it with solvent.

GWR OPEN

The Ratio plastic kit for the GW 12-ton open wagon has been around for a good few years now, which is as much a tribute to the quality of the kit as it is to the continuing demand for all things Great Western. It is a model of Diagram O29, of which several thousand were built in the early thirties, but bears a family resemblance both to its predecessors and to all GW-designed opens up to and beyond nationalisation. For many years such vehicles were distinguishable by the $1\frac{1}{2}$ width plank half way up the sides or by the separate half plank that succeeded it. Later wagons were built with 10 ft wheelbase, and in many cases vacuum brakes, but were basically not so different that the kit cannot be adapted to them, as I hope to show.

Built as intended, however, the kit shares the simplicity of the ABS LMS wagon in having the axleguards moulded integrally with the sides, there being only five major parts including the floor. The corners are mitred, but the end of the solebar locates positively in a pocket at the rear of the headstock, so only the right-angle between each side and end needs to be judged visually. In any case the floor can be used as a template, and guarantees that the result will be square – though I found it necessary to trim a little off both width and length to get the two side and end assemblies to mitre correctly when sticking them together. An accurate mitre is important for the appearance of the thing; although filing a slight radius on the corner plates is prototypically necessary, it can't hope to disguise a bad joint.

The slight oversize of the floor apart, the kit went together well. Though I had

W118334 is a Diagram O29 wagon like the Ratio kit. In service, however, it has acquired a few minor modifications, some sections of half planking on the end and beyond the side door, and straps over the capping irons. The position of the label clip is unusual for an open wagon.
ROYE ENGLAND

W122983 represents Diagram O31, the next development of the wooden-bodied open: 10ft wheelbase, exposed floor boards, square-ended headstocks, and, on this diagram only, a narrowed side door, 4ft 5in instead of 4ft 7in. The remains of the pre-1936 side lettering have been outlined in chalk for photographic purposes.
ROYE ENGLAND

to drill out the holes in the backs of the axleboxes slightly so that the flanges on the top-hat bearings sat snugly up against the lip of the holes, the resulting end float in the pin-point axles was minimal, and no adjustments were necessary. The only modifications I would suggest are to replace the door springs with metal ones, since I've found that the plastic ones tend to get broken in service, and to fit new brake levers and guards. The latter in particular are pretty basic and look nothing like the GW-pattern toothed rack with which these wagons were built. In this respect alone, the kit is perhaps showing its age.

Anyone who fancies incorporating a few modest variations could do worse than look at the photograph of W 119949 in *Pre-Nationalisation Freight Wagons on British Railways.* As far as I can see, only three modifications need to be carried out to the Ratio kit to recreate this vehicle as running in the fifties or early sixties. Most obvious is the substitution of the two bottom planks at each end with steel channels; this was a common modification to these and other wooden-ended open merchandise wagons, designed to prevent damage caused by heavy goods, particularly steel, moving around during shunting. On the model, the two bottom planks (strictly, the bottom plank and two-thirds of the wider plank above it) need to be cut out before assembly between the corner plates and the vertical stanchions. Cut a piece of 10-thou plastic to fit between the sides and just to overlap the headstock below and the bottom of the half-plank above; scribe a horizontal groove in the centre, slightly round off the inner top edge, and fix on the inside of the wagon over the three holes cut in the end moulding. Now on the outside add a one-millimetre wide strip of 10-thou on edge in the centre of each hole, and if you wish, similar strips of 5-thou along the bottom reveals – the top flanges are virtually invisible.

W 119949 also has a separate half-plank on the bodysides, unlike the kit, so this needs to be scribed on at this stage. The ends have already been catered for by the previous modification. Lastly, the wagon has acquired a series of steel loops or straps over the capping strips that run the length of the top edge of the sides and ends. Most manufacturers and modellers (and I'm no exception) omit this capping strip, but the

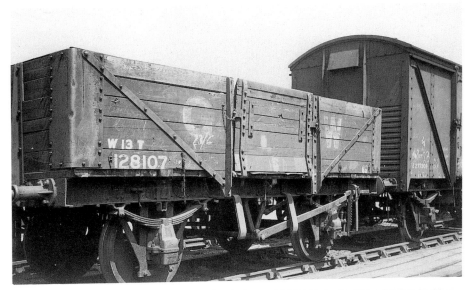

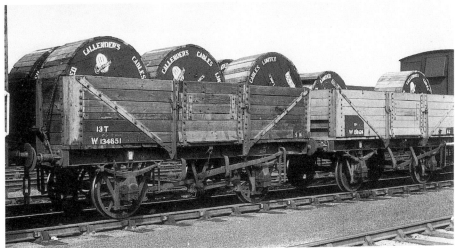

All four wagons in these photographs are to Diagram O32, the largest batch of 5-plank opens produced. The side diagonals extend below the body sides, together with modifications now apparent to the solebar-to-body brackets. The doorway is now 4ft 9in wide, and narrower corner plates are fitted to all except W128107. Only W137120 has received floor plank retaining plates on the bottom edge of the side-sheeting, and W138624 has been fitted with steel channels in its ends. Various planking and livery variations will be noted: only one wagon has been fully repainted in BR livery, while W128107 and 137120 are still in GWR colours except for the addition of a capital W – unusually placed in the case of the first-mentioned – and the obliteration of the small GW above the capacity on 137120. ROYE ENGLAND

Another early Diagram O32 wagon with wide corner plates. The large pre-1936 lettering is still visible, as it is on the vehicle next to it. This appears to be an LMS Diagram 1895 open, identical to the D1666 design except for the angled bottom plank in the side door and 10ft wheelbase. ABS produce both variations in kit form.
ROYE ENGLAND

fitting of these retaining straps was a distinctive (post WW2?) modification to many earlier vehicles, and a standard provision in BR days. The number and position of the straps varied, there being three or four on each end, and six or eight on the sides. W 119949 has four on the ends and six on the sides, plus a continuous metal strip doubled over the tops of the side doors; this appears to have been an original design feature which is already reproduced on the kit. For the small loops I cut a series of 1 mm-long rectangles of 5-thou about half a millimetre wide and stuck these in the appropriate places on the inside and outside of the sides and ends, flush with the top edge. I then added similar-sized bits of 10-thou across the top of them, and when they had set, I filed these down slightly to produce the flattened U-shape of the original.

Strictly speaking, each of these loops should have a rivet, or more properly a nut and bolt, showing on each side, but I contented myself with adding only those made necessary by the scribing of the separate half-plank. Riveting (to give it its popular name) is a tedious job best left until construction is complete, unless of course you want to do it by embossing from the rear as with metal sheet. My experience is that styrene doesn't lend itself to embossing in this way, however, and I prefer to add the rivets later by floating them onto the outside. Take a piece of 10-thou sheet and cut from it a short length

Diagram O33 was similar to O32 except for vacuum-fitting from new; they therefore received axleguard tie-bars and instanter couplings as well. According to the diagrams, they were also equipped with tarpaulin bars, but W 135941 seems not to have been so fitted, or has lost it on subsequent repair, perhaps at the same time as it acquired BR axleboxes. Incidentally, production of different diagrams overlapped; the first O33 wagons came out in 1934, the same year that saw the last construction of vehicles to Diagram O29.
ROYE ENGLAND

about the same width. Using a sharp blade, and preferably a dark sheet of cardboard to work on, slice off the end of this strip the tiniest noggins of plastic you can see; these will generally be between 5 and 10-thou thick. Try to keep these separate from each other on the work surface, because the next job is to pick each one up at a time on the point of a relatively fine brush charged with solvent and to deposit it in the appropriate place on the model, manoeuvring it into its exact position with the end of the brush itself, or with a fine tool such as a needle in a pin chuck. When

you're satisfied with a strip, give them another wash over with a brushful of solvent; together with painting, this helps to ensure that they are properly fixed and to round the profile of each one off a little so that they are not too obviously small cubes of plastic.

So much for W 119949. However, I decided to go further and convert the wagon to a later version. I chose W 144142 of which I had taken a photograph at Bedford in 1984, by which time it had acquired Oleo buffers and LNER axleboxes. I concluded that these were modifications, and I didn't feel bound to copy them. Not so the 10 ft wheelbase and fitted brakegear which, together with the alterations already described, were at first glance the only variations from the kit. Others came to light from careful examination of the photograph: square-ended headstocks, not angled ones, diagonal side bracing that extended below the body sides, L-shaped angle iron beside the doors instead of T-section, and a different pattern of support bracket between body sides and solebars. A study of *A History of GWR Goods Wagons* produced a few more subtle variations between Diagrams O29 and O37, of which W 144142 was an example, having originally been built without vacuum brakes. Most obvious of these was the absence of a curb rail, exposing the ends of the floor planks; the corner plates were shallower because of this, and were also reduced in width from twelve inches to nine. Lastly the door openings were two inches wider, but I left well alone here.

Conscious that some of this detail work might turn out to be rather delicate, I tackled the major surgery first before assembly: the conversion to the longer wheelbase. Now you might do this by substituting a 10ft wheelbase underframe kit, and so would I if I'd had one handy. But I didn't, so I took the scenic route. This involves amputating the axleguards complete with springs and axleboxes and moving each one 2 mm further out. Rather than make the incision below the lower flange of the solebar and risk damaging the spring shoes, I made the cut immediately above the flange, which not only gives the separated units a bit more strength, but also makes the joint itself stronger and easier to disguise when you stick them back in their new position. With each unit I also cut out 2 mm of flange on the outer (headstock) side, which I then separated from the rest of the unit and used to make good the gap on the other side when the axleguard was re-attached. Provided your measurement is accurate, the axles will end up parallel to each other and at right-angles to the axis of the wagon, but it's wise to check by comparing the two sides against each other from all angles before the solvent dries out. When you're satisfied that all is true, reinforce the joints by sticking four strips of 20- or 30-thou plastic (black for pref-

Few wooden-bodied open wagons survive today, and those that do are too often in this sort of condition. Although it's an ex-LNER vehicle, E277212, photographed at March in August 1991, shows some interesting detail common to the breed, including the steel channel section replacing the two bottom planks of the end, extended buffer bases of the type fitted to the LNER steel open, radiused corner plates, and straps over the capping irons. The profile of the end stanchions is rather unusual, however.

erence) behind the axleguards in line with each leg of the W.

This description only holds good in entirety of course for an uncompensated wagon. If you wish to replace all the W-irons with etched metal ones you can just cut the moulded ones off beneath the solebar. Then you have the choice of using cast springs and axleboxes, or carefully filing the moulded axleguards off the back of the plastic ones and re-using these. Slavish attention to detail demands that the kit's four-leaf springs should be replaced with five-leaf ones for later wagons, but if you choose to re-use the existing ones it would probably be wise to cut off a section of the bottom flange of the solebar as well, as previously described, to protect the delicate spring hangers. You will also need to separate the axleboxes from the springs, or the springs from the hangers, at the compensated end of the wagon. The latter is easier to do, and because the cut is in the vertical plane and a minimal gap is sufficient to ensure free movement, the result is virtually invisible when the wagon is standing on a level surface. If, on the other hand, you can contrive to detach the axleboxes complete with the front part of the saddle on the top in which the spring locates, *and* to provide a degree of clearance between them to allow the box to float up and down, the gap will effectively be disguised completely. A third, but in my opinion less satisfactory option is to file away enough of the spring hangers to leave a measure of travel between them and the underside of the solebar; the result is both rather too visible and a bit flimsy for my liking.

I then turned my attention to the detail differences on the wagon sides and ends.

Altering the headstocks was a simple matter of two cuts with a knife at each end; fortunately the overall length of the square-ended headstocks coincided with the length of the bottom edge of the angled ones. With the sides, I carved and filed away the solebar-to-body support brackets, the outer flat face of the angle iron beside the door, the diagonal strapping and a millimetre off the bottom and outer (riveted) edges of the corner plates. The corner plates on the ends need narrowing as well, of course, and this increases the width of the outer holes required for the steel channel inserts, if you're modelling a wagon with this modification.

Having removed the old detail, the first jobs were to continue the horizontal scribing of the planking across the gaps and to scribe the verticals between the ends of the exposed floor planks. These were actually slightly recessed, and a few thou should be scraped or filed off the surface of the curb rail first. This done, I added the flat strapping with 5-thou strip and the extensions of the projecting angle below the body sides with 10-thou for strength. The new diagonals are bolted to a flange on the support brackets, themselves fastened behind this downward extension of the vertical bracing beside the doors. The brackets themselves were made of two pieces of 10-thou, the rather puny right-angled joint between them strengthened with a fillet of 10- or 15-thou material inside the angle where it can't be seen. This enables the outer corner of this angle to be filed slightly round when everything has set. A third support bracket was fitted midway between these two consisting rather more simply of a flat bracing strip running from the solebar to the underside

Three photographs of the Ratio GWR open with the various changes outlined in the text. Diagram O37 was very similar to O33 pictured earlier, although originally built in unfitted form. One possible omission is the absence of plates fitted to the side sheeting to retain the floor planks. These would have been provided during BR days, and W144142 certainly had them later in life. The making and fitting of these is described under the heading of the SR 8-plank wagon in Chapter 3.

of the floor. A strip of 10-thou suffices to represent this, plus a square of the same material where the strut was bent upwards and bolted to the solebar. Finally the new strapping and modified corner plates were re-riveted.

Since the kit is designed to produce the 9 ft wheelbase unfitted wagon with brake shoes on one side only (the side with the Morton clutch), the conversion requires new brakegear. I used ABS cast 10 ft fitted brakegear, and on this occasion I removed the solid safety loops and substituted new ones from brass strip, epoxied into $\frac{1}{32}$ in holes drilled in the cast mounting block. You can use either the V-hangers moulded onto the solebar or cut these off and attach the cast ABS ones to the face of the mounting block before assembly. The ABS bits don't include a cross-shaft, so I made one up from paper-clip wire clipped into blind holes drilled in the back of each V-hanger. The cross-shaft dictates the position of the vacuum cylinder, so have a dry run first, threading the operating lever onto the shaft and locating the other end in the cylinder. You will need to remove some of the moulded underframe members from the underside of the floor for the cylinder (a job best done at a much earlier stage in the proceedings, as I soon discovered), and you may also have to adjust the angle of the lever to get the cylinder to sit squarely. You can then epoxy the cylinder, lever and cross-shaft in place all at one go. Note that the cylinder on these wagons is always (apparently) left of

A comparison of modified and unmodified wagons built from the Ratio kit. The Diagram O29 vehicle is painted in immediate post-nationalization style, with 'GW' replaced by 'W' in front of the number, and all other lettering retained.

centre close to the side without the Morton clutch when viewing the wagon from that side and the right way up.

I mentioned earlier that I felt it worthwhile to replace the brake levers supplied with the kit. Fortuitously, a set of Masokits parts for 10-ft Morton brakegear had recently come to hand, which includes not only suitable levers, but also an etching for the distinctive GWR toothed rack and round-topped guard. This is etched in one piece, and is slightly simplified as a result, so I ended up using only the racks themselves and soldering these edge-on to my own guards bent up from brass strip, which saved the ultra-fiddly job of cutting my own teeth (to coin a phrase). It also enabled me to file the lip at the top of the rack which retains the lever in the off position, and which is not provided for in the etching.

Door springs were formed from more brass strip a little over 1 mm wide, with a tongue enabling them to be set into holes drilled in the solebar. This is to be preferred because experience has shown that they tend to get knocked off in service if merely glued to the outside face of the solebar. So for each one I drilled two $\frac{1}{64}$ in holes at one millimetre centres and then joined them by drilling at an angle and carefully working the drill bit in and out with the pin-chuck to form a horizontal slot.

The wagon was completed with axleguard tie-bars from even more brass strip, RCH fitted stock buffers from ABS (short rib uppermost), Maygib instanter couplings and paper-clip wire vacuum pipes.

LNER 13-TON STEEL OPEN

Several years ago, the last time I built the Parkside kit for this vehicle, I went to some trouble to adapt the unfitted underframe to represent the vacuum-fitted version with LNER clasp brakes. Now the kit comes with a re-designed underframe in exactly this form, and modifications would be necessary to produce an unfitted wagon.

When they were introduced in 1945, these vehicles were a radical departure from any high-sided open merchandise wagon previously produced by the LNER or anyone else. Although some unfitted ones were built (many with planked side doors), far more were vacuum-braked from new in the style of the current kit, and BR went on to build further batches, initially with only minor detail differences (position of label boards, design of axleguards and axleboxes, etc), but later with more substantial changes, including a shock-absorbing version. However, not all the company-built wagons were identical either; the most obvious variation was the adoption of internal recesses about two-thirds of the way up the sides and ends. These accommodated rings to which ropes could be tied, and accounted for a series of characteristic circular bulges on the outside. These are not featured in the kit, but some of the vehicles (E 280209, for instance) included in the number sequences quoted in the instructions did have them, so some care is necessary here. E 282036 and 283170, on the other hand, didn't. The two main sources of infor-

mation on these wagons are Peter Tatlow's book *A Pictorial Record of LNER Wagons*, and an article by the same author in the July 1977 issue of *Model Railways*.

The first thing I noticed on looking at the sides was the rather overscale depth of the rounded horizontal stiffener along the top of the body sides and ends. Scaling off at about four inches, this is more or less double the size of the original, and it's tempting to file down the tops of the sides accordingly. Unfortunately these are just about dead to scale in height, so the stiffeners have to be reduced by filing and/ or scraping from below. They should be repeated on the inside, except on the doors, but the overscale thickness of the sides makes this impracticable.

The bulges, if you're modelling a wagon with these, have to be added to the sides. They were about six inches in diameter, and I began by laminating together a couple of 2 mm wide strips of 40-thou plastic, making sure that I filed away any burrs on the inside edges so that there was no air gap between them to weaken the joint. When this had set, I filed the resultant 80-thou square strip into a round rod, and then filed a flattish domed end onto it. With a sharp blade I chopped this off as close to the end as possible while maintaining a flat, circular base of the full diameter. This I achieved fairly successfully once I stopped the blade veering off at odd angles, and a quarter of an hour's work produced a dozen usable examples which I attached to the body sides with

Most of the non-vacuum-fitted wagons of this type received planked wooden doors as illustrated by 279034. The wagon is branded 'High Steel. Not to work off LNE System', but they were soon in common use throughout the country. Door and brakegear apart, it illustrates several of the points made in the text, such as the size of the top horizontal stiffener, the solebar-to-body brackets, door springs and buffers.
ROYE ENGLAND

solvent. When they were dry I faired the edges in as best I could with a rat-tailed file, and then drilled the corresponding dimples on the inside face of the body parts. The one photograph I traced showing the inside of one of these wagons illustrates what I take to be the standard fitting for the rope rings: a small fixed loop towards the top of the depression, with a larger, loose ring hanging from it. These were simulated with scraps of 10-thou strip, teased into a tight spiral by drawing it between thumbnail and finger, and then coaxed into an even smaller radius circle when softened with solvent on fitting.

As far as I can tell, all the BR-built examples showed this feature, although with slightly flattened, rather than rounded, domes. BR also put the end label boards on the opposite side to the LNER; the kit has them in the correct position for earlier wagons, but the style of board in the kit (plain, with bolt heads in each corner) was not fitted to all LNER-built examples, many of which featured removable ones that could be slid on and off through four clips, shown clearly in the photograph of 282036 in *LNER Wagons*. Anyway, 28029, which I had decided to model, definitely had boards of this sort, so I filed the bolt heads away and added the thinner flanges top and bottom in 5-thou, each with a couple of short bits of the same overlapping slightly outside them to simulate the clips.

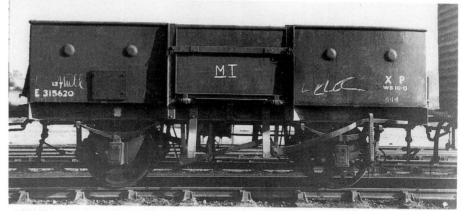

E315620 was built after nationalization and was vacuum-fitted to LNER Diagram 194. It has plate axleguards, and displays the circular bulges on the sides and a label board similar to, but larger than, that of the kit.
WESSEX COLLECTION

B486865 was built in 1952, and represents BR Diagram 1/041. It was fitted with BR plate-front axleboxes and 4-shoe vacuum brakes, although others to the same diagram emerged unfitted. This elevated view illustrates the wooden planked floor and the rope rings inside their recesses in the body sides and ends.
WESSEX COLLECTION

Before assembling the body, there are a couple more modifications to do to the ends. The first is to file off the moulded buffer bases to enable the kit's rather meagre offerings to be replaced with more lifelike ones in due course. The plastic buffers supplied are both rather undersized across the head and, more noticeably, almost two millimetres short in length: barely 15 inches overall instead of the $20\frac{1}{2}$ inches required for the fitted version of these wagons. However, even the ABS RCH fitted buffers I used as replacements needed some modification. In the first place, ABS buffers come with a very fat spigot which is fine for their own cast kits, but requires a hole of such diameter that it can seriously weaken a plastic headstock. So I generally file them down when using them on plastic kits, first filing a series of flats around each one, and then fairing the peaks away, turning the buffer round in my fingers continually. Unless you're very assiduous, you'll probably be left with a bit of a radius at the point where the spigot meets the back of the baseplate, so to ensure that the baseplate butts up to the headstock properly, I usually countersink the edges of the hole very slightly with an oversize drill bit. Reducing the girth to fit a hole about 1.5 mm in diameter is what I aim for, but if at the end of the day the odd buffer is a slack fit, you can rely on a blob of epoxy round the tail of the spigot to secure it, and at the same time to strengthen the headstock/floor/solebar joint.

I don't normally fit the buffers at this stage, however, because with some kits the solebars partly obscure the holes in the headstocks, and it's easier to file a flat on the buffer spigots if necessary than to fit the solebars around them and risk upsetting the more critical job of locating these correctly. This means that the second modification to the buffers needed on this vehicle could only be done later: the addition of the upward-projecting lug on the buffer bases similar to the floor-retaining lip on the end-door end of RCH coal wagons (ABS do produce these buffers as well, but being for unfitted vehicles, they're slightly too short for this application). I did, however, add in 5-thou the corresponding extension on the top of the drawbar face plate (coupling pocket).

A certain amount of filing was necessary to obtain a good mitre at the four side-to-end joints, and the floor needed trimming to length, and also slightly to width, before

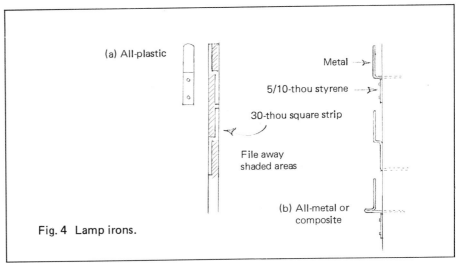

(a) All-plastic

Metal →

5/10-thou styrene →

30-thou square strip

File away shaded areas

(b) All-metal or composite

Fig. 4 Lamp irons.

it would fit snugly. This done, I turned my attention to the solebars. The top edges of these were anything but flat, and the presence of a prominent moulding line would have made a good bond with the floor very unlikely. So I filed them flat as evenly as possible, and also adjusted the length to fit neatly between the headstocks, making sure to remove an equal amount from each end so that the axle bearings stayed in line. At this stage I did a dry run to see whether, with the axle bearings fitted, the solebars would be correctly spaced for the Romford pin-point axles supplied with the kit, and whether the axles were square and true in relation to the axis of the wagon and each other. All seemed well, but harking back to my remarks about buffers, I noticed that the solebars partly covered the enlarged holes in the headstocks, so before gluing them in (one at a time to make sure that my dry run was a reliable guide), I filed a groove in the back of each end to clear a channel for the buffer spigots.

Incidentally, although I work in EM, and the wheels supplied in the kit are OO, I find Romford (ex-Jackson) wheels quite good enough in profile for finescale trackwork, and, rather than take advantage of the maker's offer to exchange the OO wheelsets for ones of wider gauge, I regauged them by gripping the axle with a pair of pliers, placing a bearing over each pin-point in turn, and tapping sharply with a blunt instrument until the wheels measured 16.5 mm back to back.

Despite the work done to flatten the tops of the solebars, I found that once they were fitted they still projected slightly below the bottom of the headstocks. I

turned this to advantage by attaching a strip of 10-thou a little over a millimetre wide to the bottom edge of each headstock, not only to make them flush with the underside of the solebars, but also to simulate at each end the bottom flange of the channel section the headstocks were made of. The mouldings lend themselves to this by being chamfered already at the back of each end. The top flange is simply a small triangle of the same strip glued to the lower edge of the body side.

Now you can fit the buffers and add the projecting lug. I cut a strip of 15-thou plastic (equivalent to the thickness of the buffer baseplates) and filed this so that the top edge was reduced to a thickness of about 10-thou. Four rectangles, each a little over a millimetre long, were cut from the strip and stuck centrally above the base of each buffer guide. The top rib on the guide extends upwards onto the lug at its inner end, and with a bit of trial and error I cut out four small triangles of 10-thou with the upper (long) side slightly dished, and attached each of these end-on to one of the lugs. Since the bottom edge is not glued to the cast rib on the guide, there is no strength in this tiny scrap of styrene, but it isn't in a particularly vulnerable position and should survive normal use.

Slightly more exposed are the lamp-irons attached to the extreme right-hand end of each headstock. For this reason it would probably have been prudent to make these from metal strip, bending up the bottom end to slot into a hole drilled in the headstock. However, I filed them out of 30-thou square plastic strip, reducing the thickness to about 10-thou on

Just about every modification under-taken to the Parkside LNER 13-ton steel open is visible in this shot, including reprofiled brake levers, the angled faces of the axleboxes with their pressed steel covers, vertical lugs on the bases of the buffer guides, solebar-to-floor brackets, side bulges and door springs. The light has just caught the area of body side where the depth of the rounded stiffener along the top edge has been reduced.

opposite sides above and below the centre. To make them even more susceptible to damage, a short length of 10-thou strip was then attached so that it projected horizontally for the lamp to sit on.

Vacuum pipes were fashioned in my usual way from paperclip wire. These are a rather strange omission from a kit designed to be built as a fitted vehicle, particularly an LNER one, so many of which had that company's tall, angled pipe mounted above the coupling hook. 280209 was so fitted, although some, including 282036 and 283170 mentioned earlier, had them at buffer level. Note that whereas it was normal for pipes in the lower position to be to the left of the drawhook as viewed at both ends, the general arrangement drawing of LNER standard fitted underframes reproduced in *LNER Wagons* indicates that the high pipes emerged on the left-hand side at one end and the right-hand side at the other – in other words, that the pipe didn't cross over somewhere under the wagon. The drawing shows the pipe on the opposite side to the vacuum cylinder, and photographs suggest that this was generally, although not exclusively, the pattern. However, it was certainly true of 280209, a fact that I failed to notice until it was too late. The retaining straps near the top of the pipes were each made from three pieces of 5-thou strip: two were stuck to the surface, one on either side of the pipe, and the third, pre-curved by rolling the tip of a round file over it on a sheet of softish card, clipped over the pipe and inside the others.

The body was bracketed to the solebar in three places on each side, none of them

reproduced in the kit. Each of the two vertical angle-iron stiffeners was attached by asymmetrical plate brackets, the inner side at right-angles to the solebar, the outer set at about 45 degrees. Together with the flanges where they are bolted to the solebars, these were represented by 10-thou plastic. By good fortune, the backs of the stiffeners have slight recesses moulded into them below the body sides which serve to make a good corner joint for the outer end of each side of the brackets. Incidentally, I felt that the chamfer or cut-away of the webs of the stiffeners at their bottom ends was not distinct enough, and remedied this with a few strokes of a file: it should equate to virtually the full depth of the projection of the stiffener below the side.

The third bracket is a much simpler affair consisting of a length of strip running diagonally from the centre of the bodyside below the door to the bottom flange of the solebar. A short piece of 10-thou will do for this.

The plastic door springs supplied with the kit don't really do justice to the shape of the original, nor to the rather unusual fitting by which they were bracketed clear of the face of the solebar – in most cases, at least. Some early vehicles had them cranked to clear the bottom flange and bolted directly to the solebar, as with the GWR open. Once again, metal strip was the only satisfactory material, and in this case I simulated the visible bottom leg of the U-shaped bridge-piece that holds the spring off the solebar by an L-shaped piece soldered behind the top of the spring. The projection thus formed was filed down to make a spigot that fitted a $\frac{1}{32}$ inch hole

drilled just above the bottom solebar flange, into which it was in due course to be epoxied. In fact, I didn't fit the door springs until after the brake gear; when I did get round to it, I also added the two bolt heads which actually attach each one to its bridge-piece. I made these from rounded 20-thou plastic strip and just Mek-ed them to the metal – not a very reliable joint, I know, but once again they're relatively well-protected, and a coat of paint will help to secure them.

The axleboxes are clearly intended to represent the LNER cast steel variety, but fail to reproduce the characteristic angled front which slopes in towards the top. This is fairly easy to put right with a file and a couple of bits of re-applied detail, but the wagon I was modelling had boxes with pressed steel fronts, which weren't flat but raised with recessed edges. So I cut four rectangles of 10-thou slightly smaller all round than the face of the box, and having filed the faces back at an angle, stuck each one onto the middle of its box; when dry, I rounded the outer edges and made a stab at fairing in the inside ones with a round file, before re-applying the handle at the top with a short length of 10-thou strip and the bolt head on the bulge at the side with rounded 20-thou.

The moulded clasp brakes needed a bit of cleaning up before fitting: the top edge of the carrier to ensure a good bond with the floor, and the brake shoes because they tend to be thicker at the back than at the front, though this means that the shoe hangers should now be bent in a little to bring the shoes as close as possible to the wheels. I also drilled the centre of each shoe $\frac{1}{32}$ inch to take a yoke of 30-thou plastic rod once the mouldings were fitted, and finally added safety loops of 26 swg wire.

The vacuum cylinder included with the kit is too small in diameter by about a millimetre, according to all the drawings I checked, so I replaced it with a Kenline cast one, which comes complete with actuating lever. The rounded top of the cylinder needs to be filed down quite a lot to bring it to the right level and to give a nice flat surface to mount it on the angled pad on the underside of the floor. I substituted the plastic cross-shaft with one of $\frac{1}{32}$ inch brass wire clipped into blind holes drilled in the backs of the relevant V-hangers (strictly, the back of the single V-hanger on one side, and the back of the angle-crank of the cross link that connects the two V-hangers on the other side). Proper holes would have made a better job, but the plastic is a bit thin to take them.

This left only the brake levers and guards. The ones supplied with the kit are a bit flat and representational, and on another day I might have replaced them with metal ones. However, I decided to try to reprofile them with plastic overlays,

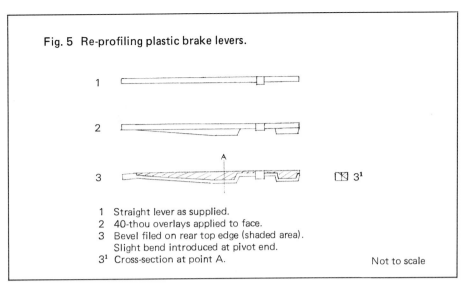

Fig. 5 Re-profiling plastic brake levers.

1   Straight lever as supplied.
2   40-thou overlays applied to face.
3   Bevel filed on rear top edge (shaded area).
         Slight bend introduced at pivot end.
3¹   Cross-section at point A.   Not to scale

and added pieces of 40-thou strip to the shaft and handle of each lever, allowed the joints to set, and then filed away the rear faces at an angle to give a fairly thin top edge without destroying entirely the strength and integrity of the original moulding. The piebald, unpainted result looks pretty awful, but at least the shape is more realistic, and a coat of underframe muck will hide a multitude of sins.

Finally, to attach the levers more strongly, I stuck a short strip of 30-thou to the solebar so that the top of the guard was fixed to rather more than just the edges of the top and bottom flanges; and partly for the look of the thing, but also because it strengthens the job, I added the strap that secures the bottom of the guard to the axleguard by putting reverse bends in a small strip of 10-thou plastic.

BR SHOCK OPEN

Three of the Big Four developed their own design of shock-absorbing vehicles, and while Parkside's recent release of kits for the BR open and van-bodied versions was a welcome break into a market untapped since the demise of K's LMS open some years ago, it covers only a small part of the potential.

Shock wagons were born out of a need to protect delicate goods like china and glassware from the rigours of loose shunting. Instead of being rigidly attached to the underframe, the body was allowed to float backwards and forwards within the limits of rubber-mounted springs on the solebar. The earliest examples appeared in the thirties, and at least a dozen different designs of vans and opens followed up to about 1960; the most modern were in use for steel traffic until very recent times, and may still be. Although at first glance they looked like ordinary vehicles, they were shorter in the body and distinguished by three vertical white stripes (blocks after 1964) on the sides and ends, and were normally marshalled at the head of a train when loaded.

The Parkside kit depicts the BR standard design fitted with sheet rail; it is thus a Shocbar (or Shock Hybar, or just Shock; codings varied, it seems, according to the whim of the building or repair shops involved). It represents the batch built in 1956 numbered B 724275 to 724674. The only photograph I tracked down of one of these was one I had taken in Warrington in 1984 of B 724371; having reached pensionable age, it had lost its sheet rail, had different axleboxes and buffers from the kit, and had acquired various other modifications including end steps below the solebar and grab handles to suit. The nearest approximation to the kit was the photograph of B 724032 in *British Railways Wagons* (Plate 20), and even this has different buffers and axleguards. So, trusting soul that I am, I decided to model the wagon as the makers intended, albeit adding some extra detail such as capping straps and label boards, with which they all seem to have been fitted, and replacing any parts I felt to be sub-standard.

Taking this last point, the kit is, in truth, a bit like the curate's egg: good in parts.

Except for a bit of flash, the body details are crisply moulded, and the recessed steel corrugated ends are nicely reproduced, together with the vertical planking on the inside. By comparison, the underframe is a bit of a disappointment, though happily capable of improvement. In particular, the axleboxes bear only a passing resemblance to the split type commonly fitted to BR vehicles, the vacuum cylinder is a poor misshapen, undersized thing, the brake levers are moulded straight except for the cranked handle end, and the brake shoe assembly, although correctly handed for Morton four-shoe brakegear, is miles too short: the shoes end up a good millimetre from the tyres of scale wheels.

Having stuck my neck out like this, let me also quickly say that the post WW 2 modeller would be in a poor way without the Parkside range, from which, with a little bit of trouble and an eye to modifications and adaptations, an impressive series of vehicles can be produced.

The sides and ends are butt-jointed, and the mouldings incorporate slight rebates which interlock with the adjoining part, a combination ideal for maximum strength. The floor is oversize by about 0.5 mm in both length and breadth, but a few strokes of a flat file cope with this. I fitted U-shaped loops over the top edges of the sides, (but not the ends, which, being steel, didn't have capping strips), as described for the GW open; curiously, these are shown on the line drawing in the instructions, but omitted from the mouldings themselves.

I modelled the tarpaulin bar in the lowered position, though it is capable of being fixed in the raised one, in which case the wagon would normally not travel without the tarpaulin itself. The arrangement of the bar around the pivot points on the wagon ends is a little simplified, but I contented myself with filing flats on the bar itself over the last 8 mm or so from the pivot to about the mid-point of the triangular plate that was intended to fill in the hole left when the wagon sheet had been properly tied down. I also added scraps of styrene to represent the brackets by which the plate was fixed to the bar. Incidentally, the line drawing shows the bar as having sharply-angled corners, but photographic evidence points to these normally having been more gradually radiused over a foot or thereabouts. The drawing also exaggerates the width of the three white stripes on the body sides: it would be dangerous to say that none was ever so painted, but the stripes were typically about four inches wide until the advent of the post-1964 short, fat ones.

Because the body is shorter than the underframe, a few inches of the main members of the underframe are visible at each end. These are reproduced in the kit by projections on a sub-floor to which the headstocks have to be attached; the headstocks are a bit thick for the steel channel of the original, perhaps for strength, so I chamfered the rear edge with a file to reduce the apparent width at the top where it was visible. This meant that I had to create a matching chamfer on the ends of the underframe members, which resulted in the underframe being short by about half a millimetre over the headstocks – less than I had expected, and a virtually undetectable compromise.

Even without this, the solebars would have been rather overlength, and needed thinning at each end – by an equal amount, of course, otherwise the axles will be askew. Before fitting them, however, I cut and filed off the rather nasty axleboxes

and springs, and replaced them with MJT RCH ones, which needed minimal attention to reproduce the plain front of the spring saddle on those fitted to B 724032 and others. A dry run proved that with pin-point bearings fitted, the solebars were exactly the right distance apart when butted up to the edges of the sub-floor.

The brake assemblies were lengthened by the simple expedient of cutting them in two: divide the base roughly in the middle and cut out the tumbler that connects the two push-rods. A 40-thou plastic flitch plate stuck to the inside of the base fixes the two halves about 2 mm apart, (they can be adjusted so that the shoes just clear the wheels while the joints harden), and the tumbler is then refitted – fortunately the push-rods are long enough to enable this to be done. A strip of 10 thou

stuck to the rear of the tumbler, long enough to overlap the rods at each end, makes a more secure job of it. I then fitted a cross-shaft of 30-thou plastic rod and a Kenline vacuum cylinder and actuating lever, home-made brake levers soldered to Masokits brake guards, and door springs of brass strip. Because the solebar is encumbered with the shock-absorbing equipment, the door springs on the real thing are fastened to the rear of the solebars rather than the face, and I sandwiched mine between the solebar and the base of the brake assembly. Lastly I used scraps of round and flat styrene to simulate the ends of the mountings of the shock-absorbing gear where these rather conspicuously protrude from behind the fashion plate which hides the gear proper.

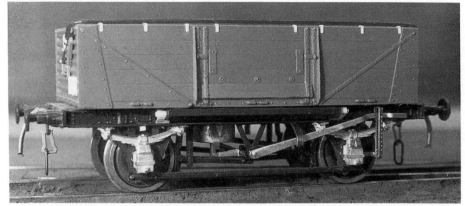

The extent to which the body of a shock wagon was shorter than the standard 17ft 6in underframe is shown by this photograph of a completed Parkside kit. The other obvious difference from normal opens is the cover-plate on the solebar which largely, but not quite, hides the shock-absorbing gear.

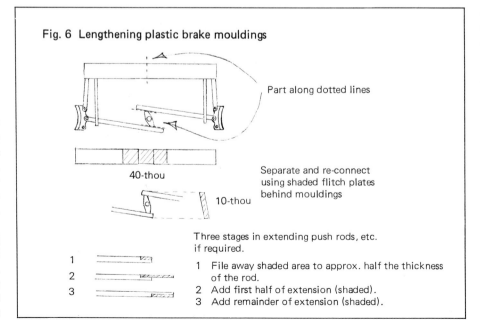

Fig. 6 Lengthening plastic brake mouldings

Part along dotted lines

40-thou

10-thou

Separate and re-connect using shaded flitch plates behind mouldings

Three stages in extending push rods, etc. if required.

1 File away shaded area to approx. half the thickness of the rod.
2 Add first half of extension (shaded).
3 Add remainder of extension (shaded).

SR SHOCK OPEN

So far we have looked at open wagons produced by BR and three of the Big Four, leaving only the Southern. As far as I know, no kit exists for a Southern five-plank open, and frankly its similarity to those built by the other companies, especially the GWR, makes this unsurprising. The Southern did boast a distinctive eight-plank vehicle used for both merchandise and mineral traffic to a design inherited from the pre-group era with both side flap and top cupboard doors; two kits are available for this, but we shall deal with it under the heading of mineral wagons, and consider instead another recognisably different Southern design, Ashford's shock-absorbing wagon that was produced both before and after nationalisation. Incidentally, drawings of all three are available in the range marketed by Mike King (see bibliography in Volume 2).

What makes these wagons different from other shock opens, and, indeed, from most ordinary opens, was the height of the sides, which was increased by virtue of the fact that the ends of the floor planks were exposed above the bottom framing of the body. At the end, in fact, they were six-plank wagons, though only five-plank ones at the sides. They also shared with some LMS-designed shock wagons a line of prominent angled stiffeners below the side door. In the absence of a kit, scratch-building is the only option for the body, although a commercial underframe may be used with some adaptation. Principally, this involves the altering of the headstocks to include a representation of the frame members visible outside the ends of the body as per the Parkside kit. My own model used the underframe for the Ratio Southern 12 ton van, with Morton four-shoe vacuum brakes, as illustrated by the photograph of S 14042 in *Pre-Nationalisation Freight Wagons on British Railways*. Mike King's drawing shows the rather more complicated design of vacuum brake gear peculiar to the SR and perpetuated on the early examples produced under BR auspices.

The sides and ends of the body were made of 30-thou styrene sheet, scribed inside and out with a scraperboard knife to represent the planking. This operation was done with the pieces marked out end-to-end on a single sheet of plastic so that

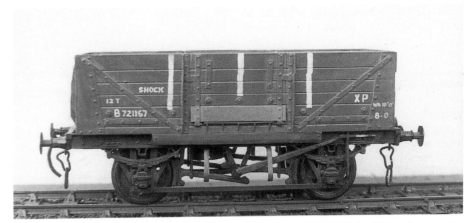

Similarities and differences between the SR-designed shock wagon and the BR product can be seen by comparing this vehicle with the previous photograph. Unlike the vast majority of standard opens, many shock wagons were rated at only 12 tons carrying capacity.

at least three out of the four corners would match exactly. If you're going for butt joints, rather than mitred ones, reduce the width of the ends when marking out by the combined thickness of the sides. Having cut the four parts out, you can choose whether to detail them now or after assembly. It's six and half-a-dozen, really, but I prefer to do it before sticking sides to ends because I find it easier to handle them while they're still flat. In addition, by overlapping the part of the corner plates attached to the ends by the thickness of the sides, you can contrive a rebated joint for additional strength and to guarantee the consistency of each corner in terms of the position of sides and ends in relation to each other.

The first element of the detailing is the angled bottom plank of the side door, a feature of all later open wagon designs intended to ease the lot of porters barrowing goods onto and off loading platforms. Chamfer the edge of a sheet of 30-thou material, reducing the thickness evenly over the width of the plank – about 3 mm in this case. Cut this strip from the main sheet and attach, filed side down, to the body side. Strictly speaking, this is incorrect, of course: the angle of the plank was visible on the inside as well, and to be absolutely accurate the plank should be cut out of the side and replaced with a new one cut to size with the top and bottom filed slightly obliquely. Alternatively, having allowed the overlay to dry, you can file a corresponding chamfer on the inside, taking care not to stray beyond the edges of the door opening.

The support brackets beneath the side doors consist of a length of strip the same width as the bottom of the angled plank (30-thou) together with a series of small triangles cut from the same strip. All of these are set on edge, and if we are working strictly to scale, should probably be cut from 5-thou sheet. For vulnerable projections like these, however, I prefer to use 10-thou, restricting the thinner material to those sections of ironwork that are attached flat to the surface. So the end stanchions, for example, consist of 2mm-wide strips of 5-thou stuck to the wagon end, to which shaped 1.5 mm-wide pieces of 10-thou are attached on edge. Similarly the L-angle beside the doors are strips of 5-thou with webs of 10-thou butted up to them. Incidentally, one of the few body differences between the SR and BR batches of these wagons was that BR changed the T-section of the end stanchions to U-section. I failed to notice this when building my own model, and have wrongly numbered it as a BR diagram 1/035 wagon (for which it should also have different axleguards); one of these days I must re-number it.

These wagons were equipped with the Southern's own style of circular rope cleats on the sides and ends. These were made from two sizes of disc cut from the end of 20- and 40-thou square strip which had been rounded with a file. With a bit of practice, discs of 5- to 10-thou thickness can be pared away quite consistently, the smaller discs attached to the body side and the larger ones on top of them, finishing off with a central fixing bolt as part of the final riveting operation (see the GWR open). White styrene is infinitely better than plastic rod for this kind of detail: the rod is harder and more brittle, and difficult to cut into very small pieces. It is, however, suitable for use as door hinges, for which short lengths are attached to the underside of the horizontal stiffeners beneath the side doors, to be overlapped by the 5-thou verticals of the hinge straps proper.

Finally, once the body has been assembled and attached to the underframe, the cover plate that hides the solebar-mounted shock-absorbing springs can be made. These were basically flat, and flush with the body side, but the bottom edge was turned under slightly, and for this reason the plates should be made from 20-thou material, chamfered at the bottom and thinned down at the ends to represent sheet metal. A spacer of 40-thou or similar

stuck behind it mounts it the correct distance off the solebar.

With this and other wagons involving the simulation of strapping or ironwork on the sides and ends, the use of 5-thou styrene is an important feature. For several years this was difficult to get hold of, but it is now fairly readily available again, marketed under the Evergreen label, and whilst it still tends to be the province of more specialist suppliers, it's worth hunting out for its value for all kinds of intricate detailing. You can use 10-thou as a substitute in most cases without seriously impairing the appearance of the finished product, but remember that this scales out at $\frac{3}{4}$ inch, which is very substantial iron-work indeed, and, strangely enough, seems to look heavier when applied flat than it does on edge.

One form of styrene that I don't use, however, is ready-cut strip: this is rarely

the exact size you want, and whatever people may say, cutting strip to precisely the required width from a large sheet is not difficult, given a good straightedge and a sharp blade. Admittedly the thinner gauges have a tendency to curl away from the line of the cut, but never in my experience to the extent that it can't be straightened by drawing it between your fingers a few times. Another thing to watch whenever you cut styrene sheet is that the knife throws up a burr on each side of the cut, which, if left, catches the light when facing outwards, or causes an air gap, resulting in a suspect joint, if turned inwards. Always, and I mean always, file or scrape the edges square, or even slightly round: knife edges are rarely found on anything but knives. This is especially true of corner plates, which invariably had a slight, but visible, radius on them.

LMS MEDFIT

Although it had been quite a widespread design in pre-grouping days, and was to be perpetuated by British Railways, the medium open ('three-plank') goods wagon was, in the years prior to national-isation, almost exclusively the province of the LMS, who constructed over 10,000 of them. By contrast, the GWR built two!

Kits for the LMS vehicle are currently available from Ratio and Parkside, and I opted for the former, which can be constructed either as an unfitted wagon or as one built as such and retro-fitted with vacuum brakes by BR. For although there were substantial numbers built new with vacuum brakes, they all featured the LMS style of underframe equipped with clasp brakes and long springs with J-hangers at the ends. Until recently, anyone who fancied this variant was forced to scratch-build much of the running gear, but the recent release of Parkside's separately-available PA16 chassis kit is a welcome solution to this difficulty. It also eases the lot of someone building the steel-bodied derivative of the LMS Medfit built in quantity by BR, the majority of which were similarly fitted.

In common with their BR-built descendants, these wagons were in wide-spread use until very recently, having passed into the service fleet once their days in traffic had ended, where their full-length drop sides were a useful asset.

Rather surprisingly, I could find only two photographs of these wagons in their BR vacuum-fitted form with Morton 4-shoe brakegear: one appears in *An Illustrated History of BR Wagons* and shows a BR-ordered example with different axleguards and axleboxes from the kit; the other I took myself in Edinburgh in 1984, and even this was built in 1949, though to an LMS order, and has the BR axleguards to prove it. Examination of my photograph of M 480626 shows a few other differences as well: 20-inch buffers, as befits vacuum-

braked stock; the inevitable straps over the capping irons; and minor modifications to the ironwork on the sides and ends. Nothing, however, that couldn't readily be incorporated into the kit during construction.

The first thing I tackled was the substitution of angle-iron strengthening for the flat outer strapping on the wagon ends, a modification shared by all the later vehicles. Since this is marginally nearer the edges, the moulded ironwork needs to be filed off, and the replacement, which extends to cover the headstocks immediately outside the buffers, built up in plastic strip – 5-thou for the flat bits, and 10-thou for the projecting webs, which are chamfered top and bottom. If you're going to fit longer buffers, make sure you leave room for the bases, which may be slightly wider than the ones moulded on the headstocks.

Being fitted, these wagons sported lamp irons on the ends. These were fabricated as described for the LNER steel-bodied open, and attached to the bottom plank about 2 mm to the right of the left-hand buffer. Other photographs suggest that a position about the same distance to the right of the drawhook was more common, however.

The modifications to the wagon sides evident on M 480626 were also common to newer vehicles. Wagons built from about 1937 onwards featured a piece of vertical strapping, to which the door control mechanism was attached, extending over all three planks, whereas earlier ones were only one and a half planks long, as per the kit. This was easily replaced with 5-thou strip. Slightly more complicated was the change to the door-stop arrangements at each end: pre-war wagons had a wooden block bolted inside the channel of the headstocks on which the sides rested in the lowered position. From about 1945 this became a piece of angle iron, and a metal loop was fitted to the sides to prevent the timber making direct contact with the stop. Once again the kit represents the earlier version. The moulded wooden block was cut back so that it barely protruded beyond the end of the headstock, and was then reduced in size top and botton: rather more at the top where there is a distinct gap of about three inches between the stop and the upper flange of the headstock channel. I used the edge of a thin flat file to cut the plastic back at an angle between the stop and the flange so that only the edge of the headstock was visible. A small rectangle of 10-thou plastic was then stuck to the face of the wooden stop overlapping slightly towards the centre of the wagon. The metal loop was filed from square 30-thou strip in much the same way as the lamp irons, removing two-thirds of the thickness of the strip above and below the loop to make the attaching brackets, and then filing away from the rear between these brackets to form the loop proper

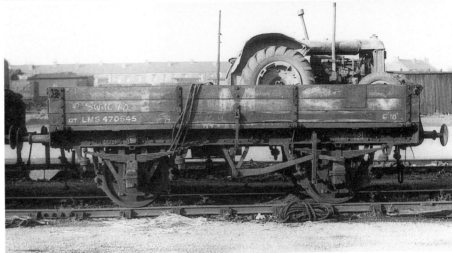

The two fitted wagons pictured here date from 1935, and feature the long springs with auxiliary suspension at each end, and the short brake levers characteristic of LMS fitted vehicles. They bear identical bodies to the Ratio kit, however, and could be produced by replacing the underframe with Parkside's PA16 kit – slightly complicated by the fact that the Ratio solebars are integral with sections of the floor, but quite feasible all the same. The two unfitted wagons were built in 1937 and show the earliest of the changes mentioned in the text involving the mounting of the door control mechanism. These and all later wagons, therefore, require some modification to the kit, which represents the first few batches produced. ROYE ENGLAND

The upturned remains of standard LMS medium goods wagon M478332, one of a batch of 500 ordered in 1946 and fitted with LMS-style vacuum brakes from new. Although damaged, and stripped of wheels and axleboxes, a lot of the gubbins that normally remains hidden from view is revealed in these photographs. Brake rigging, vacuum cylinder, springs, door control mechanism and framing are all visible. So, too, are all the modifications to the body introduced during the period of construction of wagons to Diagram 1927, which spanned fourteen years. Final livery, incidentally, was red and grey.

with daylight visible through it when fixed to the body side.

Then, once the capping straps had been added, the sides and ends could be assembled. The instructions recommended building up the body around the floor/underframe unit, but for reasons noted elsewhere I prefer to tailor the floor to the body rather than vice-versa. In this case, in fact, the floor proved to be about 20-thou too narrow, and had to be packed out with 10-thou strip down each edge to provide proper support for the sides (which are correctly spaced according to the dimensions given in *An Illustrated History of LMS Wagons*). The floor unit is relatively unusual in design, in that the solebar mouldings incorporate a strip of the floor, and are glued to the outer edges of the main floor section. This makes for very precise spacing of the axleguards, which, with bearings fitted, proved to be spot-on for standard 26 mm axles. Unfortunately, it also tends to leave a couple of rather prominent joint lines running lengthways a couple of millimetres or so inside the sides, and the strips of floor visible between these and the sides have no planking moulded in. When the joints have set properly, therefore, you need to file the surface flat across the joint lines, and then re-scribe the planking over the full width of the floor.

If you're careful about attaching the solebars to the floor you won't make the same mistake as I did and get them slightly out of line in the vertical plane, (there are locating pips to help you get them square to each other horizontally). As a result, when I inserted the wheelsets I got a slight, but definite, rock with the wagon standing on a flat surface. It's times like this that you realise the value of not cementing axle bearings into their holes. Removing the one that seemed low, I worked a 2 mm drill bit around in the hole, trying by degrees to enlarge it in one direction only. After a few minutes there was enough play in the fit of the bearing to eliminate the rock, and only now did I fix this one bearing in place with a drop of solvent.

At this point I set about altering the axleguards to the BR style, which is solid below the springs except for various combinations of horse or capstan hook holes. Small, wedge-shaped pieces of 20-thou plastic were glued into the angles of the W-irons from the rear so that a flush surface was presented to the front. When all was dry and set hard, I drilled out the holes $\frac{1}{32}$ inch round about the bottom of the inserts.

The spring-loaded door control levers were fitted next, as per the instructions; anyone modelling the LMS-pattern batch ordered by BR should note that, according to the picture of B 457203 in *An Illustrated History of BR Wagons*, this was fitted to, rather than beneath, the solebar, as also with the later steel-bodied version.

Brakegear, too, was fitted according to the instructions, except that I incorporated a cross-shaft of 30-thou plastic rod which is omitted from the kit. EM/S4 modellers need to reduce the thickness of the moulded boss that butts up to the bottom of each V-hanger so that the brakeshoes line up with the wheels. The brake levers are quite respectable, but I did add the stay bracket at the foot of the guard, and also stuck a short length of 20-thou to the handle end of the lever, and chamfered away the top rear edge behind it once the joint had set.

One or two modifications remained. The tie-bar between the axleguards (which should be removed for unfitted or clasp-braked vehicles) is a bit thin, I believe, for the flat strip variety fitted by BR. It's also very delicate and liable to break in service, or at least when handled, and so I replaced it with flat brass strip about a millimetre wide. Experience has shown that these too can occasionally come adrift in use, but at least they can be Evo-stuck back on again very quickly.

The buffers supplied with the kit are alright for an unfitted wagon, though, like the tie bars, they are liable to get broken in service, I've found. However, the vacuum-fitted wagons received longer buffers (sometimes by the simple expedient of welding a two-inch collar round the end of the guide), and I used ABS RCH fitted stock buffers once again.

The body was attached to the solebars by a couple of triangular plate brackets below the two central side-door hinges. These were cut from 10-thou sheet, each one three millimetres-and-a-bit by two millimetres-and-a-bit. The angles by which they were actually bolted to the solebar and floor were cut from the same material; it should be noted that they face the centre of the wagon. What appears to be a vestigial bracket moulded onto the middle of the solebar should be removed.

It's not possible to tell from my photograph what sort of couplings were fitted

The Ratio LMS Medfit, built to represent the final lot ordered before nationalization. All the modifications mentioned are illustrated here, including the infilled axleguards.

to M 480626. LMS-built fitted wagons all seem to have had screw couplings, and although it's possible that some or all of the retro-fitted ones had instanters, I nevertheless used PC etched screw couplings on the model, although on reflection these should perhaps have been type B with the fixed tommy-bar. When assembling these I find it useful to drill out the etched holes in the links to about half a millimetre, otherwise they tend not to be loose enough to work freely. The same goes for the hole in the drawhook that the top link slots through, and which it can easily bind on in the horizontal position. Unless all the parts can move freely the coupling tends to jam up and can then sometimes pull apart.

BR MEDFIT

Although not quite so prolific in their output as the LMS, British Railways built over 4,000 medium goods wagons, most of them to a new, all-steel body design which, except in dimensions, owed more to the contemporary plate wagon than it did to the traditional three-planker. If the body was new, however, the underframe was not, and more than three-quarters of them used the LMS clasp-braked fitted underframe, the remainder being given RCH 4-shoe vacuum brakes. No kit has ever materialised for this vehicle, even though their transfer at a relatively early age to the engineer's fleet gave some of them a lifespan of forty years or so; if you want one, scratchbuilding is the order of the day, but some assistance is now available thanks to the Parkside kit for the LMS fitted chassis.

The principal challenge to the scratchbuilder is the thinness of the steel sides. I have commented elsewhere on kit manufacturers' tendency to produce steel-bodied vehicles of elephantine proportions, which presumably has something to do with a perceived need to build massive strength into them, but fortunately the scratchbuilder is not obliged to follow suit. Nor does he have to resort

to sheet metal to obtain the characteristic profile, though this would be a perfectly acceptable way of doing it. Provided the wagon is not going to get excessively rough handling, 20-, or even 15-thou plastic is quite thick enough to remain straight, certainly on a vehicle whose sides are no more than 8 mm high, and aided, as it will be, by a good deal of exterior framing. To judge from drawings of these and similar steel-sided wagons in *An Illustrated History of BR Wagons*, the top flange was three to four inches wide. If we assume 50-thou, therefore, and allow 5-thou for the flat interior bracing, the use of 20-thou for the basic side leaves an overlap of 25-thou clear of the sides, which becomes the width of the bracing applied edge-on to the outside – except on the ends, where it was more like double this width anyway, cut away top and bottom, and itself strengthened by additional strip steelwork welded to the outer edge.

All the bracing fixed flat to the sides and ends, except for the side door hinges, is 5-thou material. Hinge straps, and the bracing that is edge-outwards, including the top flange, is 10-thou. Where T-section is used on the ends, the 5-thou is attached first, and the 10-thou stuck to it;

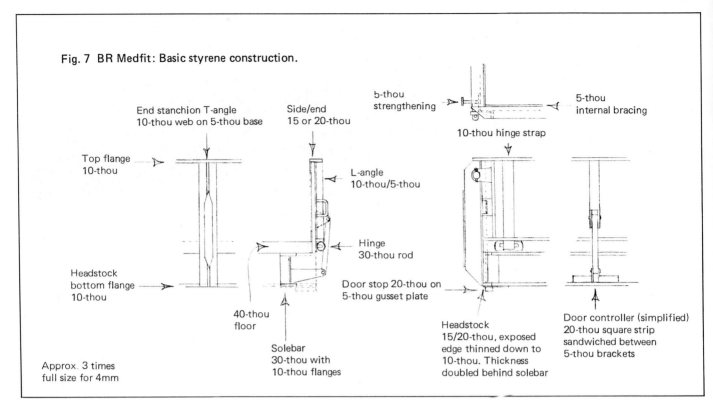

Fig. 7 BR Medfit: Basic styrene construction.

End stanchion T-angle
10-thou web on 5-thou base

Side/end
15 or 20-thou

6-thou
strengthening

5-thou
internal bracing

10-thou hinge strap

Top flange
10-thou

L-angle
10-thou/5-thou

Headstock
bottom flange
10-thou

Hinge
30-thou rod

Door stop 20-thou on
5-thou gusset plate

40-thou
floor

Solebar
30-thou with
10-thou flanges

Headstock
15/20-thou, exposed
edge thinned down to
10-thou. Thickness
doubled behind solebar

Door controller (simplified)
20-thou square strip
sandwiched between
5-thou brackets

Approx. 3 times
full size for 4mm

L-angle can be made either way round, with the 5-thou being butted up to the 10-thou webs which are put on first, or vice-versa. With such relatively thin material as 20-thou, strong corners are more difficult, but the 5-thou internal bracing can be used to make rebates, albeit minimal ones, which at least give a positive location, and slightly more than a plain butt joint. If you omit the outer T-section stanchions on the ends until the body has been assembled, they can be used to cover and strengthen the joint between side and end, assuming, that is, that you have arranged for the sides to overlap the ends, which somehow seems the natural way to do it.

Label boards are rectangles of 10-thou, with the vertical framing at the sides made from two narrow ($\frac{1}{3}$ mm, or thereabouts) strips of 5-thou, one stuck to the body alongside the board and the other to the face of the board itself. Side door hinges are noggins of 30-thou plastic rod stuck to 3 mm-long strips of 5-thou, and the door fasteners (which can only go on after assembly) are two bits of 20-thou square strip, rounded with a file, sandwiching a 10-thou hasp. The reason for not using plastic rod in the second case is that it tends to be too brittle to make very small pieces.

Going back a stage, obviously, when marking out the sides and ends, the headstocks should be incorporated. Reduce the

depth of the headstocks by 10-thou to enable the bottom flange of the channel section to be added later, and reduce the height of the sides and ends by the same amount to allow for the top flange. The headstocks will need to be thickened up to a minimum of 40-thou; the width of this reinforcing should be tailored to the distance between the solebars to give a good corner joint for them to sit in. On the real thing the gap between the rear faces of steel solebars was 6 ft 3 ins (25 mm), although on the model you may have to adjust this slightly according to the design of underframe and fittings you intend to use. This is pretty much a matter of trial and error, I'm afraid, but if 25 mm turns out to be too much you can always thin down the rear corners of the solebars, and if it's not enough you can pack them out; what will decide it will be the spacing of the axleguards, on which the free running of the wheelsets so critically depends.

Before reinforcing the headstocks and adding the bottom flange, assemble the sides and ends and fit the floor. This can be located by the horizontal internal bracing strips in the same way that the vertical ones provide rebates for the corner joints. Floor thickness is not really critical, but the surface of the planking was level with the continuous framing close to the

bottom edge of the sides (i.e. the bottom of the side door), so 40-thou is about right, and also lends rigidity to the model. Now you can thicken up the headstocks, and add the lower flange in 10-thou strip. The upper flange is simply a little bit of the same, though slightly narrower, stuck to the underside of the floor hard up against the rear of the headstock. Cosmetically, the exposed edge of the headstock should be reduced from 20-thou to 10-thou by filing a bevel on the inside.

When I made my model of B 458293 as pictured in *BR Standard Freight Wagons*, there was no alternative to scratchbuilding the underframe as well as the body, at least if you wanted the clasp-braked version. With the advent of Parkside's chassis kit there is now a way round this, but since I expect to be dealing with this in Volume 2 when talking about the vans for which it was specifically designed, for now I shall stick to describing the home-made sort, which in any case should still be useful in other connections. The solebars are the first step. For most common-or-garden 12 or 13 ton steel underframe wagons, and Medfits are no exception, these were nine inches deep and formed from channel section which was slightly more than three inches wide across the webs. Now you could no doubt use brass section for these, but if you're going to stick with plastic

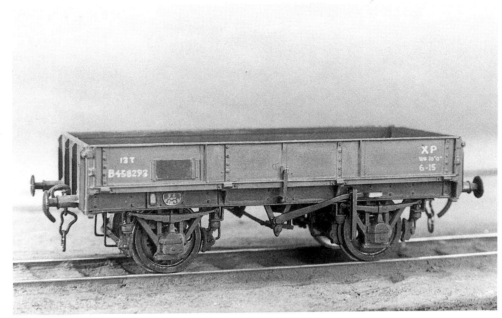

B458293, a 1951-built medium open goods to Diagram 1/019, with LMS-style fitted underframe. The manner of construction of the body follows the principles illustrated in the diagrams opposite.

you've got an immediate compromise to make in the interests of producing a reasonably solid job. I wouldn't be tempted to use anything less than 30-thou for the solebars, cutting a strip 2.5 mm wide from a sheet long enough to give you both of them. Try to produce a square rather than an oblique edge; file the edges square if necessary, because the next step is to add the webs or flanges of the channel from strips of 10-thou. This is where the compromise comes in, because to reproduce the appearance of the channel on the outside, these strips need to be appreciably wider than $3\frac{1}{16}$ inches; I would suggest that something between 50- and 60-thou ($3\frac{3}{4}$ to $4\frac{1}{2}$ inches) is about right. Stick one of these strips to each edge of your piece of 30-thou, which will deepen the finished article to 3 mm. Try to make sure that one edge of the 10-thou is flush all the way along with the rear face of the 30-thou. On most wagons you can in fact get away without the top flange, which is virtually invisible under the floor, but it's nice to know it's there.

Cut and trim the solebars to length to fit snugly into the rebates in the backs of the headstocks. As far as you can, make sure before you glue them in that they will be the right distance apart to accept the spacing of whatever axleguards you are going to use, whether these are cast metal, etched brass or plastic, or a combination of some sort. Not that there is any great mystique about this: you won't be far wrong with your prototypical dimension of 25 mm, but remember that because of

the compromise just described, the faces of the solebars will already be half a millimetre or so further out on each side than they should be, so try not to exceed that distance, and reduce it if at all possible.

Once you've taken the plunge and fitted the solebars you can add visible details: number plates, label clips and brackets. On the BR Medfit these took the same form as on the LMS version (not surprisingly since it was the same underframe), including the triangular gusset plates beneath the solebar/headstock joints. The door control levers are also the same, except that they are bracketed to, rather than beneath, the solebars. Whatever you make these of, they are delicate and rather vulnerably positioned; I feared the worst when I used 20-thou square strip, bracketed top and bottom by pieces of the same sandwiched between overlays of 5-thou which extend to enclose the ends of the bar. So far, however, they have stood up to several years of operational use, so they can't be as delicate as all that.

When it came to the axleguards, the only ones at the time that came anywhere near were Kenline part 31b, which do have long springs fitted with J-hangers, but also have RCH-type W-irons rather than the BR plate variety. The axlebox itself isn't a perfect match, either, but with white metal castings alteration is not easy, and the only alternative was scratchbuilding. So I convinced myself that the Kenline ones were near enough, and married them to clasp brake castings from the same source, drilling out the centres of the shoes

first to take yokes of $\frac{1}{32}$ inch wire. With bearings fitted, I had a dry run to check once again whether the spacing was correct, and even though all seemed well, I still Evo-stuck the axleguards on one side only to begin with, doing another dry run with the other side to satisfy myself once and for all that the wheels turned freely without too much slop.

Safety loops from nickel-silver wire were set into squares of 60-thou stuck to the underside of the floor. With clasp brakes there were two to each yoke, eight in all, completely encircling the yokes at both ends. From a normal viewing angle only the outer leg and part of the bottom of each loop is seen, so this is all you really need to fit, and for a bit of extra security you can, if you wish, solder or epoxy them to the underside of the yokes, although in reality they weren't so attached, of course.

V-hangers can either be cut and filed from brass or nickel-silver sheet, or rather more quickly made from 20-thou plastic. The metal ones have a finer profile, and might be thought to be stronger, but by the time you've put in a cross-shaft of 30-thou plastic rod (or $\frac{1}{32}$ inch wire) and added the brake levers, there isn't a lot to choose between them on that score. Kenline again supplied the vacuum cylinder, and ABS the 20 inch buffers. Brake levers and guards were home-made to the short pattern generally fitted to wagons with LMS long spring suspension. The bottom of the guard should be braced to the nearest axleguard as usual, but in this case it goes in the other direction.

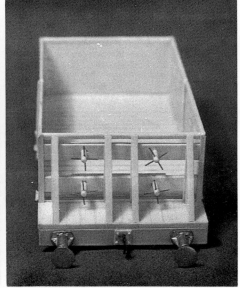

Two views of a completed body for a Palbrick A to Diagram 1/023. The relative thinness of the lift-out side panels, and the unusual design of the ends, especially the one with the securing clamps, makes these vehicles something of a challenge for the scratchbuilder.

PALBRICK

Brick traffic was carried by the railways from the earliest days, mostly in the form of loose bricks packed in straw in open wagons, including the famous GN bogie vehicles (which unfortunately didn't enjoy the widespread use that many of us would like to believe). By the 1950s the slow, labour-intensive job of loading and unloading loose bricks was causing BR and its customers to look at ways of expediting the operation; the result was the Palbrick, designed to transport bricks ready-palletised. The new system was embraced with enthusiasm, (at least by BR), and over 1,400 vehicles were built in the space of four years from 1957, including some conversions from redundant Medfits. Unfortunately, the traffic was short-lived, although some vehicles have achieved a lifespan of over 30 years by being adapted without much change into Freightliner match wagons, in which form a few still survive. Not all of BR's brick traffic was palletised before its demise, but more than one brick works in the Wrexham area dispatched its products this way, so I determined that the Brynowen Brick and Fireclay Works should do so too.

You might think that all members of a class of wagon built over so short a span of time would be the same, but not so. Palbricks exhibit in microcosm, the kind of evolutionary development that all the more common designs underwent: three different types (Palbrick A, B and C) to seven different diagrams, incorporating numerous variations in dimensions and detail, make for a rather complicated picture. Admittedly they were all vacuum-braked, and all *looked* much the same: load-carrying space shorter than their standard 17 ft 6 ins underframe, and pairs of lift-out plywood side panels between heavily-buttressed ends, one of which incorporated a set of screw clamps to secure the load. But the greater width of the B, and the clasp brakes and roller bearings of the C and later Bs were fairly distinctive.

I decided to model a rake of three, and chose two As and a B. I left out the C partly because it is barely in my period (construction only started in 1959), and partly because I had no photographic evidence of all three types marshalled together, though I had seen As and Bs mixed. Background information and drawings of both types came from *British Railways Wagons* and *An Illustrated History of BR Wagons*, and there is a useful photograph of a B in *BR Standard Freight Wagons*. Construction presented a few challenges, and the drawings needed a fair amount of interpretation, and comparison with the photographs, particularly in the areas of the central removable side stanchion and the adjustable clamps. The lack of any photograph of the inside of the wagons showing the adjusters was particularly unfortunate, but if you wait for proof of every little detail you'll never start anything, so I made a few best guesses.

Since the sides are only plywood edged with metal strip, they are particularly thin, and I felt constrained to try to reproduce this feature. I toyed with the idea of sheet metal, but didn't fancy either mixing materials or the extra work of making the whole body out of metal, so in the end I opted for 15-thou plastic sheet edged with 5-thou on each side. At just under a scale two inches, the result is a not entirely satisfactory compromise between rigidity and appearance: fairly strong, but a bit heavy-looking.

The metal edging round the body of each panel is repeated round the slots designed to accommodate the tines of a fork-lift truck. I didn't trust myself to locate these accurately on both outside and inside of each panel by measurement alone, so I first attached rectangles of 5-thou to the outside, left them to set for 24 hours, and then cut out the slots carefully in the centre of each one. I used the resulting hole to position a similar piece of 5-thou on the inside, left that to set, and then cut the slot in that from the outside, using the pre-cut edges as guidelines.

Since the model sides were not intended to be removable, the sides and one fixed end could be made as three individual pieces in the usual way. The end with the screw adjusters, however, is an openwork fabrication of channel and angle iron, and would be difficult to model separately in one piece. So before tackling this I made the floor, scribing the planking into a piece of 40-thou (transverse planks in the load area, longitudinal ones between the stanchions at each end), and attaching head-stocks and solebars for rigidity. This gave a solid platform to locate the fixed end and the sides firmly, which in turn produced a frame for the other end.

The two sections of channel in which the adjusters are mounted were made of 15-thou edged with 5-thou after the manner of a steel solebar. Pilot holes were drilled to locate the adjusters (although at this stage I wasn't quite sure how I was going to make these), and each channel sized carefully to fit snugly between the sides. I had made the angle-iron corner posts integral with the sides and allowed for a slight overlap round the end to give a corner joint for the channel pieces; again, the exact design of the corners was difficult to fathom from drawings and photographs, so I fudged it a bit.

Having fixed the channels in place, flange inwards, I made up a length of one millimetre square angle iron out of 10-thou strip to form the top rail of the end framework, and attached this in the same way. As with corner plates and any other feature where the exposed edge of a steel angle is made up of two pieces and visible on the finished model, it pays to disguise the joint by tidying it up with a file once it has set, and to round the corner slightly (very, very slightly) to avoid a knife-edged look.

Four vertical strips of 5-thou provide the mounting for the triangular stanchions that buttress the ends; these were cut from 10-thou sheet and, after fitting, 10-thou strip formed the flange on the sloping edge. That left the adjusters: the difficult bit seemed to me to be the X-shaped handles at the outer end which are used to screw the adjusters in or out, together with the horizontal beam attached to each pair that clamps the load. Wire would have had a degree of damage resistance, but to look right would have to be soldered into fine holes drilled at 90° through the screw close to the outer end. This seemed like hard work, and there was the added difficulty of fixing metal screws firmly in the plastic channels. In the end I made plastic screws of 40-thou strip, rounded with a file, and the handles of 10-thou rod inserted into $\frac{1}{64}$ inch holes in the screws. Strictly speaking, these holes should be in the same plane and meet exactly in the centre, but I drilled them just far enough apart to make the handles of two lengths of rod instead of three, maximising what limited strength there might be in the finished product. Fortunately they are partly

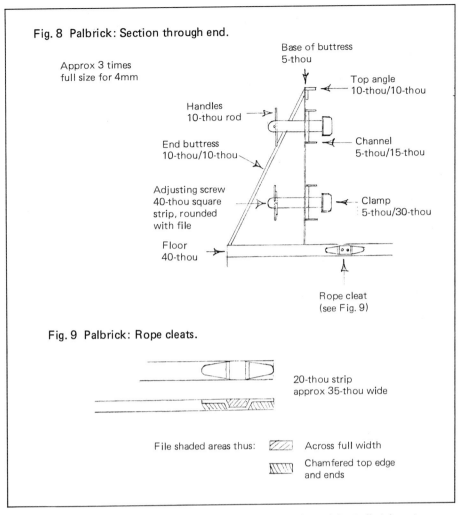

Fig. 8 Palbrick: Section through end.

Fig. 9 Palbrick: Rope cleats.

protected by the buttresses, but you have to be quite careful not to catch them inadvertently, all the same.

The rope cleats fitted to Palbrick As and Bs (though not Cs) were of the double-winged type introduced round about that time, and subsequently used on much of the fleet of air-braked open wagons. They were mounted on the edge of the floor, three to each side, and being the best part of a foot long, should not really be left off. They were formed from a single piece of metal, tapered towards each end, and bent inwards in the centre where they were bolted to the side rail. I made them from a length of 20-thou strip just under a millimetre wide, filing away the bulk of the thickness alternately front and back. Behind the wings, however, I filed at an angle, thinning down the top edge only so as to leave the full thickness lower down, and ensuring that each one could be attached to the body over more or less its full length. The taper was introduced with the blade as I chopped each one off the end of the strip.

If the bodies of the Palbrick series were unusual, the underframe and running gear were pretty standard. All of the As and most of the Bs had RCH 4-shoe vacuum brake gear, for which sets of castings are available from ABS. Axleguards were of BR pattern, available in etched form from Comet, MJT and the EM Gauge Society. Published photographs show axleboxes of either BR plate front type or, rather strangely, LNER pattern, although others were probably used as well. The former have been elusive until recently, but the Parkside PA 16 chassis kit includes not only the LMS long spring underframe suitable for Medfits, but also alternative mouldings for the BR 10 ft underframe with standard springs, BR axleguards and plate front axleboxes – which saves you the job of making solebars into the bargain. Alternatively, axleboxes of this style are amongst the easiest to make yourself from lumps of styrene, being very square and angular.

LOW-SIDED WAGONS

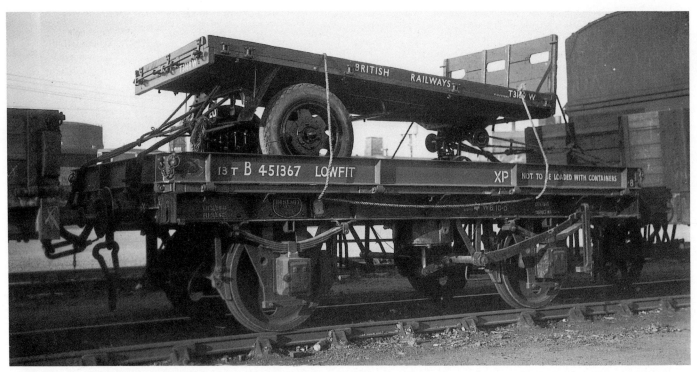

B451367 is an example of the first batch of BR Lowfits built with steel bodies, and has the LNER design of fitted brakegear that was superseded by Morton 4-shoe brakes in most of the later batches. Later vehicles also had nine vertical stiffeners in the side doors instead of the four shown here. The load is typical. ROYE ENGLAND

In railway parlance, low-sided wagons are generally those with sides, one, or sometimes two, planks high, frequently used for carrying machinery or wheeled vehicles, and often with hinged, drop-down ends and/or sides to enable them to be loaded from platforms. To a degree their function overlapped with single car-carrying wagons (the Southern Railway built vehicles very similar to the LNER and BR Lowfit, and both Carfit and Lowfit brandings have been seen on them), with runner wagons for overhanging loads, and with container-carriers. With the latter, the picture is rather confused, however. Only the LMS used one-plank wagons on any scale for containers, and they used a mixture of hinged and fixed-sided vehicles. BR and ex-LNER wagons with drop-sides and ends, being vacuum-fitted, were coded Lowfit, and were specifically branded 'Not to be Loaded with Containers' (thus, incidentally, catching out more than one ready-to-run manufacturer who has marketed a container-carrying BR Lowfit). However, some at least of the fixed-sided LMS-built wagons, many of which were retro-fitted with vacuum brakes by BR, were then also coded Lowfit and acquired

the same branding. As if that were not enough, a batch of ex-SR long-wheelbase Carfits was later used for containers and re-coded Conflat D!

Although they were relatively numerous (BR alone built over 3,000), low-sided wagons have received scant attention from kit manufacturers catering for the post-grouping scene. Indeed, the only current kit I'm aware of is ABS's white-metal LMS one-plank wagon; this is available in as-built unfitted form, or with a kit of parts that enables the BR vac-fitted conversion to be produced, but otherwise its construction follows the lines of the LMS 5-plank open already described, so detailed coverage here would be rather superfluous. Cambrian did at one time offer an interesting composite plastic and white-metal kit for the early BR Lowfit, and examples may still be around, although I haven't come across it recently. It was noteworthy for being the only kit I have seen that incorporated the straps or clips fitted to retain the capping irons along the top of the wooden body sides and ends. Apart from these, you're on your own.

Well, perhaps not quite. For a start, there are plenty of drawings available, covering the LMS vehicles (*The LMS*

Wagon and *An Illustrated History of LMS Wagons*), the LNER (*A Pictorial Record of LNER Wagons*) and both wooden and steel-bodied BR stock (*An Illustrated History of BR Wagons*). Moreover, there is a body available: both Bachmann and Replica currently offer the ex-Main-line LNER/BR wooden-bodied vehicle, which looks quite nice, and includes such detail as the rope rings set into the floor. Unfortunately, it's a scale six inches too narrow, and whilst it is possible to widen it by cutting it down the middle and grafting in strips of plastic to separate the two halves, by the time you've done this and repositioned the end detail, you might as well have scratchbuilt the thing to begin with. If you do opt to modify a body in this way, I suggest you start by sticking a strip of, say, 20-thou under the floor of one half so that it overlaps the cut over its full length (minus headstocks) by at least 5 mm. This gives you a rebate into which to set a 2.5 mm wide strip of 60-thou (2 mm for the extra width plus 0.5 for the saw-cut), and leaves enough to give a similar rebate for the other half when you stick them back together. You can't do the same at the ends of course, but these are so low that a 2.5 mm wide piece of 30-

A trio of model Lowfits. On the left the early BR steel-bodied version with 4-shoe brakes; in the centre an ex-LNER vehicle using a Mainline body married to a lengthened 3H wooden underframe, modified to incorporate LNER fitted brakegear; and on the right, the original Cambrian kit for the first BR batch with LNER-style body and LMS underframe.

thou sandwiched between the two halves will be quite strong enough. Scribe the planking across these fillets and make sure that any visible joint lines are filed and sanded away, and a coat of paint will do the rest.

A further modification is necessary to use this body for an LNER vehicle. All of these, as far as I am aware, had wooden underframes, and the sides were therefore slightly deeper and recessed at the ends around the timber headstocks. Accordingly, you should stick a 20-thou strip of plastic along the bottom edge of each side, 3 mm (i.e. two thicknesses of 60-thou for the headstocks) shorter than the overall length of the body. My model was built long enough ago to be able to use the old 3H LNER wooden solebars supplied with their open and van kits, but a present-day alternative would be the Cambrian underframe kit, which is available separately. Both are for 9 ft wheelbase unfitted vehicles, however, and both have RCH axleboxes, whereas all the LNER Lowfits I have found pictures of have the company's own design. So some extra modifications are necessary, the most important being to cut the solebars in two in the middle and graft an extra 4 mm section in, flitching the joints behind in the normal way. With the Cambrian solebars, you will also need to remove the face-mounted central V-iron, and, to be strictly accurate, the builder's plate at the left-hand end, replacing this with an LNER wagon plate, which the 3H ones already have. On the other hand, the 3H solebars need shortening at the ends, and the Cambrian kit comes complete with headstocks and buffers, so it's a case of swings and roundabouts.

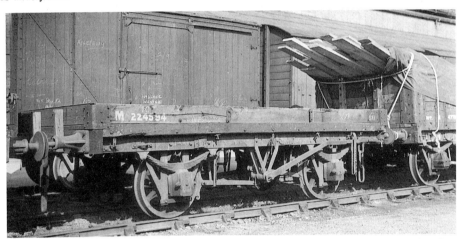

A pre-grouping, possibly ex-LNWR survivor in use as a runner wagon beneath an overhanging load in BR days.　　ROYE ENGLAND

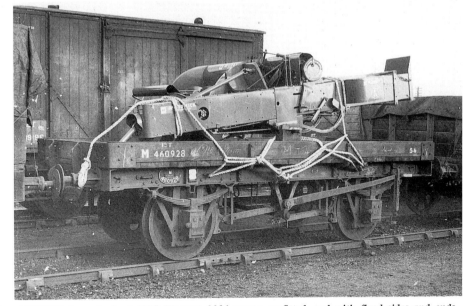

M460928 is a standard LMS Diagram 1986 wagon, unfitted, and with fixed sides and ends, though by this time sporting BR plate-front axleboxes. Others, including 460374, 460648 and 460741, were equipped with 4-shoe vacuum brakes in later life. Again, the load is a typical one for this class of vehicle. This is the only modern low-sided wagon for which a kit is currently available.　　ROYE ENGLAND

A selection of LNER-built Lowfits which between them reveal a lot of detail of the construction and fittings. Apart from wheels and lettering variations, they are all very similar. The only significant difference seems to be on E202848, which has acquired large wooden chocks on the headstock, apparently to help support the end in the raised position.

WESSEX COLLECTION

The standard form of LNER fitted brakegear was used, with three V-hangers and eight shoes – as with the steel-bodied open. The pivot-points of the two V-hangers on the non-vacuum cylinder side were 16 mm apart, and it should be noted that the V-irons themselves were asymmetrical – the leg nearest the wheels was almost vertical. I cut mine out of 20-thou plastic, which is quicker than drilling and filing them out of sheet metal, but at the cost of rather overscale thickness. But, to be honest, you have to look pretty closely to be able to tell. A vacuum cylinder from ABS or Kenline, together with clasp brakes from the same sourses, or Comet, wire yokes and cross-shaft, and homemade levers and guards are necessary to complete. Buffers are ABS RCH fitted style.

The first batch of 400 Lowfits built by BR used the same body, altered only where necessary to suit a steel underframe. Because they were built at Wolverton, however, the LMS underframe with long springs and J-hangers was used. As with the Medfits we have already looked at, the Parkside PA16 underframe kit would be suitable, (although some wagons received LNER axleboxes, it seems – B450092, at least, had this combination in 1968). For the second and subsequent batches a new style of steel body, still with drop-sides and ends, was introduced. For these, however, production was transferred to Shildon, and the first ones built reverted to the LNER fitted underframe, though this time in steel rather than timber. With the body, there's nothing for it but scratch-

building (the principles described for the BR Medfit apply), but for the underframe Parkside come to the rescue again with their PA06 kit, the one supplied with the LNER steel open. For the majority of the steel-bodied vehicles, however, it's back to PA16, but this time to the alternative

mouldings for the solebars with BR plate-front axleboxes and short springs, married to cast parts for RCH 4-shoe vacuum brakegear. Later wagons also had a slightly modified design of body side, with additional vertical stiffeners on the full-length drop doors.

Close-up photographs of two of the models illustrated earlier. The BR-built wagon has a scratch-built body on a somewhat adapted Airfix underframe; a modern equivalent would be the alternative BR-period mouldings in Parkside's PA16 kit. The Mainline/3H wagon rather obviously shows where the body has been deepened to suit the wooden underframe. Photographic evidence points to most of these vehicles having retained their LNER axleboxes throughout.

A pair of very similar looking ex-private owners, except that the one on the left is to the RCH 1923 specification, whereas the one on the right is a few years older. The older wagon has grease axleboxes, wooden door stops and longer diagonals. Apart from the thinner top plank, however, it appears to be dimensionally the same, and could no doubt be adapted from either of the kits for 1923-pattern wagons. ROYE ENGLAND

Another pre-1923 vehicle with grease axleboxes, this time with 8-plank sides.   ROYE ENGLAND

CHAPTER THREE
MINERAL WAGONS

An up freight passing through Trowell on 12th June 1948. Although it's impossible to pick out much detail at this distance, the run-down condition of the wagons is fairly evident, and probably no two are alike. Only around this time could you expect to see a haphazard conglomeration of ex-private owners which the wartime pooling arrangements had caused to stray far from their original haunts. COLLECTION R. S. CARPENTER

We come now to what has been from the earliest days, and remains, the largest group of wagons on the railway: coal wagons. The movement of coal from colliery to seaport, from colliery to industry and power stations, from colliery to almost every station in the country for domestic use, and not least to keep the railways themselves on the move, meant that the humble coal wagon, or mineral, became synonymous with goods train operation from the very beginning of the railway era.

For over a century the vast majority of this huge fleet comprised simple all-wooden open wagons with a gradually rising capacity which eventually reached thirteen tons. Apart from the predominance of hoppers in the North-East, and the development of steel underframes and bodies, mainly in South Wales initially, the standard Railway Clearing House (RCH) designs reigned supreme from their introduction right up to World War 2. At that time all such vehicles in private ownership were pooled in the national interest. The colourful pre-war liveries soon began to disappear under workaday grime and the effects of perfunctory maintenance (or the lack of it), and although the intention was originally to restore vehicles to their erstwhile owners, evidenced by the painting of the former operator's name in white on a black panel at the left-hand end of the

Evidently not long for this world, this Gloucester RC & W 6-plank 10-tonner may well have been 50 years old when photographed after the World War 2 pooling arrangements — note the owners' name repeated at the left-hand bottom corner. With one or two modifications, like the new top half-plank with its capping straps, and the odd brake blocks, Ocean 4783 is a close match for the Slater's kit of this type.

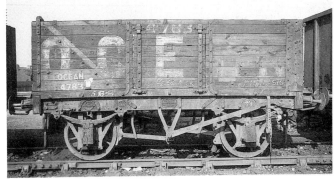

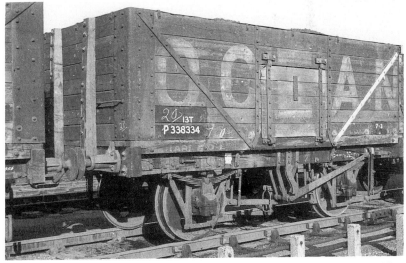

A rather more modern Ocean wagon to the RCH 1923 specification, suitable for either the ABS or Cambrian kits, albeit with a few detail alterations: capping straps, position of door protector plate, curved bottom to vertical washer plates alongside the doors, floor retaining lugs on the buffers at the fixed end (an unusual provision, possibly a make-do-and-mend repair), and end grab handles. ROYE ENGLAND

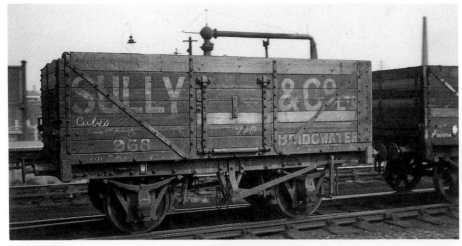

Another RCH 1923 vehicle similar to ex-Ocean wagon P338334. This one has yet to receive its 'P' number, however. The half-round wooden bar beneath the side door was not part of the hinge, but a device to close the gap between the open door and the body side.
ROYE ENGLAND

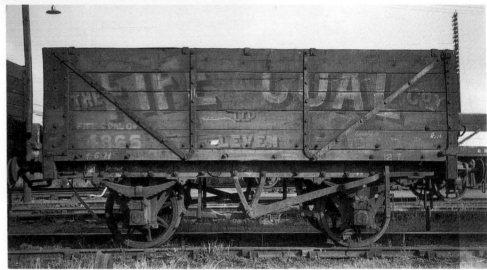

A five-plank 12-ton wagon of Scottish origin without side or bottom doors. The massive springs are noteworthy.
ROYE ENGLAND

This 7-plank 10-tonner with bottom and side doors, but without end doors (there are corner plates at both ends) appears similar to the Slater's kit for the 1907-pattern Charles Roberts wagon. Note the difference in buffer height by comparison with the fitted van next to it.
ROYE ENGLAND

body whenever the original ownership became difficult to decipher, continuing austerity followed by nationalisation saw to it that such good intentions soon faded along with the livery. After 1948 only the prefixing of the wagon number with a capital P, as opposed to the B, W, M, E and S that denoted BR and company-built vehicles, served to distinguish the former private-owner fleet – unless, that is, chance had allowed vestiges of the livery to survive, as it did here and there well into the fifties, and even beyond. For instance, a photograph in the Colour-Rail range shows 60008 on King's Cross shed in 1961 alongside an almost pristine Maltby 13-tonner. But such examples had already been rare for many years when that picture was taken.

By the late fifties, surviving wooden-bodied minerals were mostly of the RCH 1923 pattern in a livery of BR light grey or unpainted wood, or a mixture of the two. Most newly-built wagons from the start of WW2 onwards were of steel construction, and mainly of 16 tons capacity, also in light grey, and subtle shades of rust. Fitted, and/or larger wagons were at the time still greatly outnumbered by this army of primitive, hand-braked, loose-coupled stock.

On the face of it, kits for mineral wagons are quite numerous, especially if you take account of the number of different pre-printed private-owner liveries available. Anyone modelling the twenties and thirties is quite well off in this respect, with the proviso that many private-owner wagons stuck fairly rigidly to well-pre-scribed routes. However, the range of wagon types covered is actually quite small, and only someone specialising in the few years after nationalisation can legitimately get away with mixing pre- and post-1923 wooden wagons with the remains of their P.O. liveries, and Ministry of Transport, LMS, LNER and BR steel minerals, thus making the best use of all available kits for the more modern (post 1900) designs.

Right: Although this 8-plank wagon appears to be 16ft 6in in overall length, the body sides are rather lower than the two previous wagons. The cast spring shoes and (odd) grease axleboxes mark it out as a pre-1923 vehicle. Compare the longer diagonal bracing straps, and the lower capacity with the later wagons (which would have been uprated from 12 tons during the war). The pin-and-chain fastening for the bottom doors shows up well, below the solebar to the left of the V-hanger. ROYE ENGLAND

Old Silkstone No. 45 is a standard 1923 8-plank wagon, the sides of which are almost 3 inches higher than the corresponding 7-plank version. Although ABS do a kit for the LNER 8-plank mineral, this has sides which are the same height as their 7-plank wagons, so it appears that scratchbuilding would be the only option here. Note the wartime lettering and chalked amendments to the painted tare weight. ROYE ENGLAND

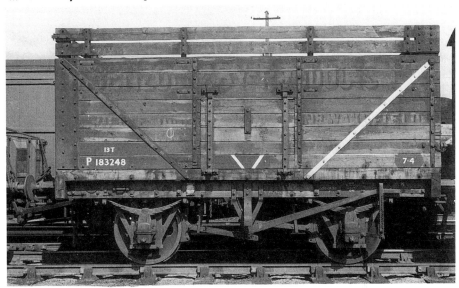

Another 1923-specification 8-plank wagon, this time with removable coke rails. ABS produce a kit for a non-convertible 7-plank wagon, with fixed rails, but here again scratchbuilding would be the only solution for the body, perhaps married to a Cambrian underframe. ROYE ENGLAND

Except for a few details, these three ex-LMS D1671 wagons are very similar, as might be expected. Variations include wheels and the position of label clips, and two of them have had the two wide top planks replaced with combinations of other sizes. M601823 has the door protector plate in a slightly different position, and is the only one to comply with the RCH drawing (and the ABS kit) in this respect. My statement that all the LMS wagons had grab handles on the end doors appears to be disproved by M341698 and M259040 — perhaps they lost them during repairs.

ROYE ENGLAND

LMS 7-PLANK MINERAL

Several variants of the RCH 1923 vehicles are available from ABS: 7-plank private owners, with and without end doors and coke rails, together with the LMS 7-plank and LNER 8-plank styles. The LNER had both 7- and 8-plank wagons without bottom doors, while the LMS stuck to 7-plank ones with bottom doors. They varied from private owners chiefly in the choice of steel T-section for the end pillars, whereas most, if not all P.O.s had wooden ones. Many of the LNER vehicles were also fitted with the company's own axle-boxes rather than the standard RCH design. I chose to model the LMS version, of which over 30,000 were built to Diagram 1671 between 1924 and 1940, not counting a further 5,700 similar bodies on steel underframes.

I found the castings for the sides and ends commendably thin, crisply detailed, and with only a modicum of flash. The only problem I had with this part of the assembly was to get the end door vertical when mated with the sides: the ends of the horizontal locking bar extend outside the door and overlap the sides, while the end door casting itself fits between the sides. However, the projections were too big to fit into the recesses cast for them, and I ended up both thinning the projections down as much as I dared, and filing a bigger recess in the sides, hoping that once the parts had been epoxied together and painted, this minor bodge would become unnoticeable.

As with open merchandise wagons, the fitting of retaining straps over the capping irons was a common post-war feature of both ex-private-owner and company-owned wooden minerals. In this case I bent these up from fine brass strip and epoxied them into place before beginning the assembly proper. I also bent a slight outward bow into the sides, a distortion acquired in service by most wooden open wagons. Lastly, I added two horizontal grab handles from fine wire to the end door: all the pre-1948 photographs I found of LMS wagons showed these, though they appear not to have been specified by the LNER, and by only a proportion of private owners.

The instructions recommend the attaching of the axleguards to the solebars before assembling the body, but committing

myself at this stage to the final position of the bearings, and thus the alignment of the axles, seemed a bit of a rash thing to do. So I put the body together first, and it was as well that I did, for I found that, having glued the axleguards to the solebar on one side, those on the other side didn't match up to the position of the spring stops cast on the underside of the solebar. I was satisfied that the body was square, so I removed the stops and, after fitting the second set of axleguards, replaced them with styrene ones in the correct position.

I also found, when I came to attach the second pair of axleguards, that the bearings

supplied were too deep for standard 26 mm axles. Fortunately, I had in stock some bearings with shallower cones which gave minimal end float in the axles. These problems highlight one of the disadvantages of white metal kits: you only get one chance to get the wheels to run true, and you can't spring them in and out after the thing has been put together as you can with plastic or etched brass W-irons.

At this point I added the wagon floor. The kit includes a rectangle of 20-thou styrene with embossed planking which needs to be cut to size. It also needs altering

Two views of the completed ABS kit for the LMS mineral wagon. The capping straps and bottom doors are clearly shown.

to include a representation of the bottom doors, unless your wagon is to run loaded all the time. Except for a line drawing showing the V markings, the instructions are silent on the subject, although all the LMS wagons had them. Luckily the embossed floor was sufficiently oversize for the offcut to be used for the doors, set into two apertures cut in the floor, and secured with a second thickness of styrene overlapping the joints underneath. Typically these doors were about 3 ft 6 in × 1 ft 10 ins and 2 ft apart. The planking ran lengthways in them, unlike the transverse planks in the main body of the floor.

The flooring as supplied is light, even flimsy; this is no bad thing in a heavy white metal wagon, but it would need some beefing-up to support a compensation unit. Alternatively it would be possible to mount this on a rigid metal cross-piece between the solebars: these have longitudinal ledges on the inside about 3 mm above the tyres of the wheels on which the cross-piece can be located. Since I was building a rigid underframe, however, I made only two very minor modifications to this part of the kit, namely to replace the rather heavy cast door springs with home-made nickel-silver ones, and to attach stay brackets to the bottom of the cast brake lever guards. Both are described under the heading of the same maker's LMS open.

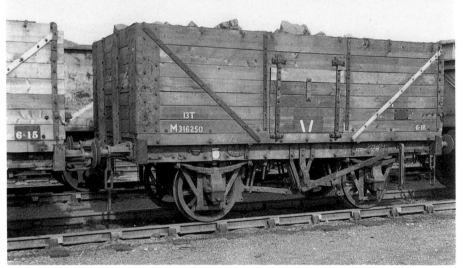

M316250 is another example of a wagon built to D1671. Unlike those in the previous photographs, it features two small angled brackets between the solebar and the curb rail close to the inner spring shoes. Relatively few of the LMS wagons had them (M603289 was another), but they were a common, though not universal, fitting on private owner vehicles. ROYE ENGLAND

RCH PRIVATE OWNER

An alternative to the ABS 7-plank private owner comes in the form of the Cambrian plastic kit, available both pre-printed and unpainted. I fancy that the body scores marginally better than the ABS model from the dimensional point of view: the ABS body sides are a little too high, not enough to look unrealistic in a train, but about $1\frac{1}{2}$ to 2 inches more than the 4 ft $4\frac{1}{2}$ ins of the original, which the Cambrian kit measures exactly from floor to top edge.

Other than the fitting of stay brackets again between the brake guards and the axleguards, this time in the form of an elongated Z filed out of a one millimetre wide strip of 40-thou styrene, I made no alterations to the kit. Some thinning-down of parts was necessary to get them to fit (the end door needed similar attention to the ABS wagon, and the projections on the buffer and drawhook baseplates moulded onto the separate headstock at that end were also a bit beefy), but the main problem was getting enough clearance for 26 mm axles. Unlike the ABS kit, where there was inclined to be too much room, the axleguards on the Cambrian wagon were just too close together, as pre-determined by the locating pips and holes on solebars and floor. Deep-coned bearings weren't enough to do the trick by themselves, and there didn't seem to be sufficient meat in the axleguards to permit countersinking to take the flange of the Kean-Maygib bearings I was using, which is often a way of getting that little bit of extra depth. Finally the answer came about by accident. I was using a small centre punch to make sure the bearings were as far in as they would go, and I must have tapped the end a little too hard, hard enough to break off the flange of the bearing, which allowed the bearing proper to settle deeper into the axlebox. Flangeless bearings are obtainable (also from Kean-Maygib, for example), though I didn't have any at the time, and I'm not sure I would recommend their use wholeheartedly: once in, they're by no means the easiest things to get out again. In this case, however, the clearance thus given between the wheel and the back of the axleguard, although minimal, was just enough to allow the axle to revolve freely without binding, but I did have to carve away a bit of the carrier on which each pair of W-irons is moulded to stop the tyres fouling it.

Once the underframe was assembled and running freely, I did what I should have done earlier, and checked the spacing of the solebars. At 6 ft 9 ins (27 mm) they are in fact about a scale four inches too narrow across the outer faces. If I were building the wagon again, I would be tempted to cut off the locating pegs on the top edges of the solebars, which fit into holes moulded in the floor, and to judge the spacing by holding the solebars in place on the ends of an axle with the bearings fitted. A bit rough and ready, but it gives you a good idea of how far apart they need to be, and you can always adjust them a bit before the joints harden.

The instructions sensibly recommend adding extra weight, especially if the wagon is to run unladen, so I Evo-stuck a piece of sheet lead about half an inch square and a sixteenth of an inch thick (scrap builder's lead flashing) between the brake assemblies. This doubled the wagon's weight to about an ounce.

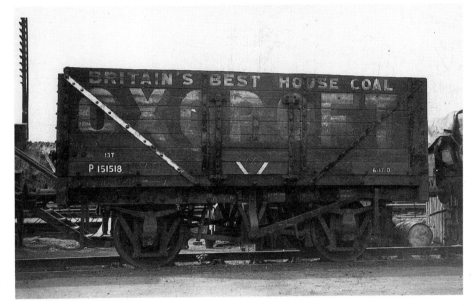

Both sides of ex-Oxcroft P151518, another 1923-pattern wagon. ROYE ENGLAND

A pair of RCH 1923 7-plank ex-private owners. The Bolsover wagon displays the wartime ownership markings, while the long vehicle has been renumbered in the 'P' series. This renumbering was apparently done completely at random, without reference to design or former ownership. Note the position of the builders' plate and label clip on the Bolsover wagon, and the shape of the top plank on P325579; Rickett was another owner who favoured this style. The two small angled brackets on the solebar mentioned in relation to LMS minerals feature clearly on the lower photograph.

ROYE ENGLAND

Three kit-built ex-private owners. At the top is an unpainted Cambrian kit, and in the centre a similar vehicle modified in the form of the Cory wagon opposite. I have to admit that I'm not sure of the origin of the wagon in the lower photograph, though it is apparently a 1923-pattern vehicle — except for those buffers. The least satisfactory thing about all three is the brake guards, which really do look rather clumsy, and the brakegear itself, which lacks something of the crispness and delicacy of the real thing.

SR 8-PLANK MINERAL

Before we leave the subject of wooden minerals, I mentioned earlier the Southern Railway 8-plank design which doubled as a general merchandise wagon. For the purpose of comparison with their RCH 1923 kit, I chose the Cambrian offering, though this vehicle too is available from ABS. The kit represents the 9-ft wheelbase version with independent either-side brakes, but the instructions are frankly rather misleading when it comes to numbering. References are given, but not everyone has access to 20-year old copies of *Model Railway Constructor*. Anyone who does, however, will find that, of the sample numbers quoted, most do not exactly match the kit as designed, particularly in the matter of brakes. The closest wagons are S 35611 and DS 26261, which did have independent brakes, and would probably have filled the bill up to around nationalisation; as pictured in *MRC*, however, they subsequently acquired two steel end channels, together with capping straps and plates to retain the floor planks. All of these modifications can be made to the kit, of course, but unfortunately, by the period I'm modelling, 26261 had also been transferred to the Engineer's Department, as the 'D' prefix implies, and converted to a cable wagon. So the prospect of its being seen carrying coal in Denbighshire seems rather slim! The fate of 35611 is unrecorded.

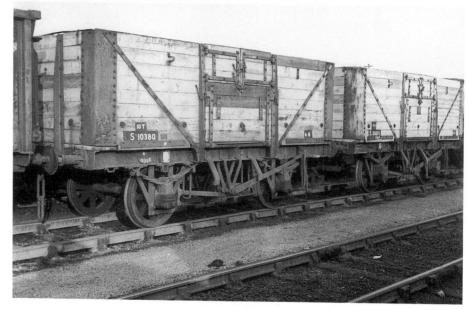

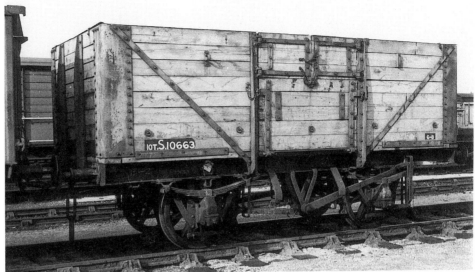

Now you may think that all this is nit-picking and finicky, and perhaps it is. The question of brakes on these wagons is admittedly complicated, and information is no doubt very patchy. At another time I might well have settled for assuming that 35611 had escaped the engineers' hands, or for modelling a vehicle fitted with Morton 2-shoe brakes, which seems to have been another common option, by cutting off the outer V-hangers and omitting one of the brake assemblies. As it happened, however, I was browsing through a copy of Mike Vincent's beautiful book *Through Countryside And Coalfield* (OPC, 1990), and there was S 10167, independent brakes and all, loading coal at Old Mills Colliery near Radstock in 1959. Not quite so far from its native turf as the Shrewsbury & Chester, but seemingly right in every other respect. The accompanying photographs show several more, all of which are fitted with floor plank retaining plates: these are referred to as common modifications in the instructions. The plates took the form of strips of metal about 3 ft 6 in by 3 in, attached with five nuts and bolts to the bottom edge of the bottom plank of the sides between the doors and each corner plate, in such a way that they overlapped the ends of the floor planks in rather untidy substitution for a curb rail. I represented them with strips of 5-thou, adding bolt heads in the usual way (to be strictly accurate, it was actually not the heads that were on the outside, but the nuts, and, despite what we call them, this was the normal arrangement. But in 4mm scale small bolts, nuts and rivets look pretty much the same in my book).

The body sides and ends are nicely moulded, although the webs of the L- and

T-section ironwork are a trifle heavy, or rather, they are wedge-shaped, fatter at the base than at the outer edge. This shouldn't matter, but all the photographs I found showed the bottom corners of each web to be cut away at about 45°, whereas they are moulded square on the kit; furthermore the top chamfer on the L-section strapping beside the doors is unusually deep, deeper than the kit suggests, extending down about five planks from the top. These chamfers are all easily made, but the modifications highlight the thickness of the material, which needs to be trimmed down accordingly by filing or scraping the sides to a thinner profile. A degree of filing is also necessary to achieve a satisfactory mitre at each side-to-end corner.

With the underframe, I again found the locating pips on the solebars and brake assemblies to be more of a hindrance than a help in getting everything properly spaced. In fact, the brake assemblies needed to be mounted at least 20-thou off

the floor to get the brake shoes to line up with the wheels, and the carrier/mounting block had to have its lower edge filed down accordingly so that it didn't protrude beneath the solebar. In trying to bend the brake levers to a more realistic profile I broke them both, so replaced them with home-made ones from brass and nickel silver; if you use the plastic ones supplied, I suggest a small block of 30-thou plastic attached to the solebar first will give a stronger joint for the top end of the brake guard.

Lastly, I also replaced the plastic door springs with brass strip, filing the inner end down to form a spigot that was a tightish fit in a $\frac{1}{32}$ in hole drilled in the solebar just above the bottom flange. The real things were bolted to the face of the solebar, so I represented this with rectangles of 5-thou strip, which also served to obscure the top half of the hole for each spigot.

SLOPE-SIDED STEEL MINERAL

The model of slope-sided mineral B6502 pre-dated the introduction of the Parkside kit which is illustrated on the right, and which has been fitted with substitute metal brakegear and additional solebar bracket work in styrene sheet. The solid cast safety loops on B9774 should be compared with the strip brass replacements used on the GW high-sided open wagon. On B6502 I made a stab at the pressed steel type of side door featured on Ministry of War Transport 7326, but failed to reproduce the raised panels between the ribs. 7326 is in original bauxite livery, which would have been replaced by BR light grey within a few years of nationalization.
Prototype photo:
WESSEX COLLECTION

As already mentioned, mineral wagon construction from the forties onwards concentrated on all-steel designs, and phenomenal numbers were produced before construction of the short wheelbase types ceased in the late fifties, sufficient, for example, to enable over a quarter of a million grease-lubricated wagons in traffic at the beginning of 1950 to be eliminated completely within seven years! Most of the later minerals built under BR auspices were virtually identical, but there was quite a variety of types before this, and one of the most distinctive was the so-called slope-sided wagon originally produced by Charles Roberts & Co. Several thousand of these ultimately found their way into BR ownership, and odd ones and twos were a common feature of steam age coal trains for twenty years or more.

An Illustrated History of BR Wagons contains a photograph and a drawing of B 9774 which had the same kind of riveted side door as the Parkside kit with simplified strapping. The kit gives you the option of the pressed steel variety of door, but I felt that this was a little crude in its representation of the original. The body sides are moulded in two sections, which are joined horizontally along the angle between the sloping lower body side and vertical upper part. To make this joint invisible, both parts need filing cleanly along the mating edges; if you don't do this, not only will the joint show, but the sides will also be a bit too high in relation to the ends. Actually, I failed to practise what I preach on one of the sides, and found it necessary to tamp a thin sliver of 10-thou plastic into an all-too-visible joint, softening the material with a plentiful application of solvent in order to fill up the crevice, and then filing it flush when it had set hard 24 hours later.

Apart from this slight bodge, the only modifications I made to the body were to make up the four short pieces of steel channel fitted vertically across the joint between body and headstock at the non-door end of 9774 (and others), and to add the gusset plates welded across each top corner, all in 5-thou plastic. These gussets highlight the fault common to almost all the plastic steel mineral kits I've come across, namely the thickness of the top edges. In reality these were only about half the width suggested by the kits, and unfortunately the normal viewing angle of the models only makes things worse.

There really isn't much you can do about this, except scratchbuild, however, and at least they all look the same.

Turning to the underframe, I found that with the solebars properly butted up to the locating lugs on the underside of the floor, there was too much slop in the axles when using standard bearings. I used bearings with shallower cones, which did the trick, but thinning down the lugs with a knife would be another route round the problem, or you could go for packing out the bearings supplied by mounting them in 10-thou plastic washers or collars made as described in chapter 1.

The brake assemblies shared with the Shock wagon the fault of being a bit too short, but this time I felt the push-rods weren't long enough to lengthen them as before. So I discarded them in favour of ABS ones, which, however, I had to file down a bit on the outer face of the mounting block to get the shoes to clear the flanges of the EM wheelsets. Having bottom doors like most other early steel minerals, these wagons had independent either-side brakes with two V-hangers on each side. The ABS castings allow for the inner V-iron to be soldered or glued to the brake assembly before fitting to the wagon; having done this, I cut the moulded V-irons off the solebar, and bent up a couple of Masokits ones to fit the outer face of each solebar, doglegged to clear the lower flange. Before expoxying these in place, I drilled them $\frac{1}{32}$ in at the apex of the V to take a wire shaft soldered into a corresponding hole in the Masokits brake levers I was using in place of the plain Parkside ones. The inner end of the shaft slotted into a blind recess drilled in the bottom of the inner V-iron in place of the cast pip which I had filed off. You

might criticize the use of V-hangers of two different thicknesses, but I'm reasonably satisfied that once painted, any visible discrepancy will be minimised.

Remaining modifications were the replacement of the kit's plastic buffers by ABS 18-inch RCH castings (the moulded

Parkside buffer heads were strangely rather prominently dished), the substitution of metal door springs for the usual less-than-impressive plastic ones, and the addition of support brackets on the solebars for both the side door hinges and the vertical stiffeners on the body sides.

STANDARD MINERALS

I commented earlier that most 16-ton mineral wagons are much of a muchness in appearance, but this is something of an over-simplification. True, vehicles built to the most common BR diagram, 1/108, outnumbered all the other straight-sided types put together, but the statement ignores the differences between riveted and welded construction, between those with or without top flap and bottom doors, and those with welded or pressed steel end and side doors, most permutations of which were produced at one time or another. Large-scale rebuildings in later years added further variations. Even so, for my purposes the similarities were sufficient to justify lumping them all together under a single heading.

There are currently four plastic kits on the market for the basic unfitted steel mineral wagon: Cambrian offer an LNER design of riveted construction and one for the LMS welded variety, while Parkside and Dapol (née Airfix) produce the BR welded pattern to Diagram 1/108. Parkside also offer a fitted version of the same, of which more anon, together with the less common 'French' and (as we have seen) slope-sided types. Cambrian's LMS vehicle claims to double as a BR one, but some care is needed here: the kit is for a vehicle without top flap doors, but the sample numbers quoted are for Diagram 1/108 vehicles, which were all built *with* top doors and only lost them on rebuilding in the 1970s. Furthermore, as the instructions point out, most 1/108s didn't have the independent double brakes featured in the kit; however, the kit doesn't supply the Morton clutch and cross-shaft needed to model the alternative. The instructions also suggest that the side with the brake-gear on was the facing side with the end door to the right; in fact, it was originally the other way round, but many vehicles were fitted with reversed bodies on rebuilding.

The nearest BR diagram to the Cambrian kit was 1/102, which had bottom doors, and therefore double brakes, and no top flaps; however, although the kit provides both pressed and welded doors, the official diagram says they were built with pressed end and side doors of a different pattern to the kit, (actually similar to the LNER design), and although some were certainly fitted with, or acquired, other styles of door, I could find in my reference sources no firm evidence of all-welded doors on 1/102 wagons in the fifties. Since I like to model specific wagons as running close to my chosen period, therefore, I played safe and modelled an LMS wagon.

No such complications exist with either of the two 1/108 kits, both of which can produce acceptable models with comparatively little extra work. The Dapol kit

retains the opening side doors that require vastly overscale moulded hinges; I cut these off, replacing them with rather more modest representations of the real thing in styrene, mounted on a square strip of 30-thou beneath the doors, and flanked by the outrigger brackets between solebar and body sides below the two central vertical stiffeners. No other major modifications were made to the body, although I replaced the end door commode handles

Not many Diagram 1/108 mineral wagons were fitted with pressed end doors, but clearly B100925, one of a batch built by Birmingham RC & W in 1952, was so equipped. Far more common was the welded type seen in the lower photograph, although in this case we are, I think, looking at a pre-nationalization wagon; it lacks the corner reinforcing of the upper one, and appears to have LNER axleboxes.

WESSEX
COLLECTION

An unusual viewpoint of mineral wagons being loaded with iron ore at Immingham in the early sixties. As well as a couple of LMS wooden-bodied wagons (M606473 and 608961 built in the late thirties to Diagram 1671), at least four different types of steel-bodied ones are visible: a Diagram 1/105 example immediately beyond M606473 — riveted construction, top flap and bottom doors, note the internal shape of the pressed end door. Nearest the camera on the middle road is M6210??, an LMS D2134 wagon of welded construction but fitted with riveted side doors; beyond it a standard BR Diagram 1/108 vehicle, and beyond that the riveted version of the same to Diagram 1/109, in this case with riveted side doors and a pressed end door. Kit manufacturers should note how narrow the tops of the sides are!   AUTHOR'S COLLECTION

Another shot of loading operations at Immingham in the sixties. Hoppers, tipplers and both steel and wooden minerals predominate, together with some 'dock use only' high-sided opens marked with a prominent white cross. The ex-LNER wooden vehicle with the low-height doors on the third road from the ship, was one of many converted to merchandise wagons during World War 2 (and not thereafter supposed to be used for mineral traffic!). Although the iron-ore hoppers are by no means full, they are loaded to capacity.
AUTHOR'S COLLECTION

At the end of the day there isn't a lot to choose between the Dapol (ex-Airfix) and Parkside Diagram 1/108 mineral kits. The replacement hinge mounting below the side door on the Dapol wagon shows where the overscale working originals have been removed.

with wire ones (hardly worth the effort, in fact: the change is barely noticeable), and tidied up the top corners to disguise the joints with bits of 10-thou, filed flush when dry. The floor was about 0.5 mm too narrow, so I stuck strips of 10-thou down each side before fitting it; even so the wagon is about 1 mm too narrow overall, and 2.5 mm so on the inside – the result of over-thick sides. By comparison, the Parkside kit is just about dead scale outside width, but for the same reason is 1.5 mm narrower inside.

I should have had less trouble with the Dapol underframe than with the Parkside: the former has more positive locations for both floor and solebars. But it didn't quite work out like that. For reasons I still don't really understand, I found it necessary to pack one end of one of the Dapol solebars 10-thou off the floor to get the axles parallel. I also had to drill out and countersink the bearing holes, even though I had thinned down the rather thick axleguards, so that the wheels turned freely. On top of that, I had to lengthen the brake moulding by more than a millimetre to bring the blocks somewhere into the vicinity of the wheels. The kit provides two mouldings, only one of which is required, and two identical brake levers; the one on the same side as the brakes should be fitted with a Morton clutch, so I discarded these and replaced them with cast ABS ones linked by a wire cross-shaft. Final detailing included the drilling of horse/capstan hook holes in the axleguards, and the fitting of metal door springs.

It has to be said that the Parkside kit can more easily be made up into a reasonable model, which is no doubt evidence of the way standards have changed since the Airfix original was introduced. Even so, the Parkside kit is not without its quirks, one of which is the absence of any positive location for the floor, which it would be easy to get cock-eyed. Another is the buffer heads, which on my sample scaled out at about $10\frac{1}{2}$ inches in diameter instead of 13; I fitted ABS standard RCH ones instead. Lastly, the axleguards are unaccountably fitted with a tie-bar, an unusual provision on a short-wheelbase unfitted wagon, and certainly not standard on 16-ton minerals.

The Cambrian LMS vehicle was modelled on M 616285 as pictured in *An Illustrated History of LMS Wagons, Vol. 1*; when photographed in 1964 it was fitted with pressed side doors and welded end door, which is an option that the kit gives you. Once again, the body needed very little attention; the floor lacks any representation of the bottom doors with which both the LMS and 1/102 wagons were equipped, but it was a simple matter to scribe these in. The underframe parts are common to several kits, evidenced by the provision of two sizes of solebar — make sure you use the shorter ones. Standard parts, however carefully selected, are rarely correct in every detail, and a minor alteration needed to the headstocks is the substitution of a square end in place of an angled one.

Once again, Cambrian's method of using moulded pegs to locate the solebars caught me out; this time, despite managing to find bearings which allowed the wheels to turn freely, (the discrepancies between different batches and makes of so-called standard bearings never ceases to surprise me), I discovered when fitting the second solebar in its intended place that the axles were slightly askew. So again I removed the pegs and adjusted the length of the solebar slightly — a little off one end and a sliver of 10-thou on the other to give a nice snug fit between the headstocks, which I had fitted first to make sure they were square. As with the Parkside kit, there is no positive location for the floor, and this time I wasn't so lucky: either for this reason, or more likely because I had failed to remove the moulding lines evenly on the tops of the solebars, the second one needed packing 10-thou off the floor at one end to get the axles parallel.

The Cambrian LMS steel mineral, showing the additional bracket work on the solebar.

Another drawback with the use of a common underframe in this case is the absence of any of the outrigger supports between the solebars and the body, which therefore need to be made up in 10 or 15-thou plastic. As seen end-on, they are T-shaped, so a rectangle of 10-thou the same width as the vertical stiffeners should be stuck under each stiffener before adding the upright web of the bracket. These are about 2 mm wide and equivalent in length to the space between the outer face of the solebar and front of the body side stiffener: 3.5 to 4 mm. The outer bottom corner is rounded, and a notch should be cut in the upper inside corner to clear the top flange of the solebar. This was the most common style of support bracket fitted to steel minerals, but the LMS wagons (and some 1/102 ones) had additional angle brackets mid-way between the outer and inner stiffeners.

As with the SR 8-plank, I replaced the brake levers and guards, but this time I retained the door springs which are just about the right shape for most mineral wagons, although I suspect they could be a trifle longer. The buffers too are pretty good, and apart from some of the heads being moulded a little off centre, they are among the best and strongest plastic ones I've come across.

I dwelt at some length earlier on the reasons why this kit could not readily be made up as a pre-1970 Diagram 1/108 vehicle. Brake-gear apart, the main problem is the absence of a top flap door. This can be remedied, of course, with a bit of scratchbuilding, and I resorted to this when tackling Cambrian's LNER kit.

Not that there is anything wrong with putting it together as an LNER-designed wagon, over 7,000 of which were built about the time of nationalisation. No kit exists, however, for the BR Diagram 1/109 vehicle, the riveted equivalent of the 1/108 design, which, although it was vastly outnumbered by its welded cousin, nevertheless reached a respectable tally of over 25,000; (by comparison, there were 200,000 wagons of Diagram 1/108 by 1960!). Since the LNER kit is the only one for a 'standard' 16-ton mineral of riveted construction, it provides the only obvious route short of scratchbuilding to a 1/109 vehicle. Now, whereas 1/108 wagons generally had welded end doors, pressed end doors were common on the riveted version. These are a lot harder to scratch-build (I know of no method in styrene other than to add roughly shaped overlays bit by bit to a flat surface and to fair them in by filing and sanding once the joints have properly hardened), but fortunately photographs of B 230009 in *An Illustrated History of BR Wagons* and B 267453 in *BR Standard Freight Wagons* both show end doors of similar pattern to the LNER style, albeit with additional strengthening above the door itself. This is quite easily added in 10-thou strip about a millimetre wide — note that the five vertical webs so characteristic of BR mineral wagons taper slightly towards the top. I also added in 32 swg wire the two small grab handles located between the outer vertical ribs about half way up the door.

One feature not represented on the kit (nor on the same maker's LMS vehicle) is the internal shape of the pressed steel doors: the inside is a plain, flat surface, whereas in reality of course the contours so noticeable on the outside were just as visible on the inside. Other than by vacuum forming I'm not sure how you would go about reproducing this, but I offer it as a not-too-serious suggestion to anyone who feels like having a go.

In the case of the two wagons quoted just now, this only applies to the end doors because the side doors were fabricated. I used the spare set of doors from the LMS kit, moving the moulded fasteners above them outwards a whisker by slicing them away carefully with a sharp blade so that they lined up more precisely with the verticals on the doors. To manufacture the top flap doors, first cut away about 14 mm of the flange (and the rivets below it) on the top edge of the body side, centrally between the stiffeners on either side of the door; when doing so, angle the exposed corners of the remaining sections of flange. Replace the flange with a strip of half-round 20-thou, obtained either by rounding the edge of a piece of sheet material and then cutting it away as thinly as possible, or by using square section strip and scraping it down once it's set hard. Strictly speaking, the same half-round profile should also apply to the inside, but the thickness of the body side makes this rather impracticable.

Next, use two pieces of 5-thou, one flat and one on edge, to make the horizontal angle-iron that strengthens the body below the top flap door. Kink the flat strip and cut notches in the piece on edge to clear the flanges of the upright stiffeners on each side. This angle forms the base on which the hinges of the flap door are mounted. The hinges are the rounded ends cut from a strip of 30-thou about a millimetre wide, on top of a short length of 5-thou (2 mm or thereabouts), and butted up to the vertical straps on the door itself; these are also 5-thou, as are the lateral lugs which fasten the door shut. The ends of the pins that the lugs close over are the rounded ends of a length of 20-thou rod – not the hard material usually sold as plastic rod, which is often too brittle to be of much use in tiny noggins like these, but a strip half-a-millimetre wide sliced from a 20-thou sheet and 'turned' with a fine flat file. If you wish to add the cotters and chains that lock the door, please do. Finally, there was a noticeable lip along the bottom edge of the door, just clear of the angle-iron; a strip of 10-thou is all that

The Cambrian LNER steel-bodied wagon with the adaptations needed to turn it into a BR Diagram 1/109 vehicle.

is needed here, and it only remains to rivet the main side doors and the strapping incorporated in the top ones.

One other modification to the body can only be completed after the solebars have been attached. On both BR and LNER wagons, the central side supports are rather longer than they are moulded, extending noticeably below the bottom of the solebars. I lengthened them by adding a bit of 15-thou on edge, strengthening this feeble effort with a piece of 20-thou stuck to the chamfered lower face of the support, shaped so that it mated cleanly with both the support and the extension piece. Once it had set, I tidied it up with a file. This left the brackets by which the extended supports are fastened to the solebar; evidence as to the exact design of these was hard to come by, but it seemed to be a sort of hollow box section. Only the bottom side of this was visible in photographs, so I contented myself with a small rectangle of 10-thou between the back of the support and the solebar, resting on the bottom flange of the solebar channel. A similar bracket was added to the shorter support at the door end of each side.

Turning to the underframe, the LNER vehicles were equipped with independent double brakes, (though without bottom doors), and for the Morton gear fitted to Diagram 1/109 it is necessary to remove the outer V-hangers, together with the mouldings on the face of the solebars (I used an old nail file with the point filed to a chisel for this). On B 267453 the remaining V-hanger was fitted with the common modification of a strengthening cross-piece just below the solebar, and this was added with a short strip of 10-thou on both sides. Unfortunately it is also necessary to discard the perfectly serviceable brake mouldings, which are the wrong way round for a wagon with brakes on the same side as the Morton clutch (the facing side with the end door to the left in unrebuilt form). I'm sure that with a bit of styrene relief work on the rear face of one of the kit mouldings, a passable result could be obtained, but I used an ABS casting which has the virtue of being reversible, with detail on both sides. Home-made levers and guards, coupled with a wire cross-shaft and a rather representational clutch (a circle of 15 or 20-thou plastic with a small dart to the right of top dead centre), completed the brakegear.

One final modification was to convert the RCH-type W-irons into the BR type, as with the LMS Medfit. B 267453 looks to have had single horse/capstan hook holes in the outer side of each axleguard, but holes on both sides were also common; others had none at all, or had odd axleguards reversed on repair, so almost any permutation is possible.

Upon completion, comparing this wagon with others, I noticed that it seemed to stand a bit high off the rails. In fact the rail surface to buffer centre distance, variously expressed as 3 ft 5 ins to 3 ft $5\frac{1}{2}$ ins (just under 14 mm), scaled out at more like 3 ft $7\frac{1}{2}$ ins on this vehicle. So too, I found belatedly, did the LMS steel mineral and the SR 8-plank, which share the same underframe. Whilst I'm prepared to put up with this in the ones I've already

built, it would cause me to investigate possible remedies when building similar wagons in future. The most likely answer would seem to be to ensure that the separate carrier on which the axleguards are moulded, which sits behind the solebar and is very precisely located by a cast pip on the solebar mating with a hole in the carrier, should be persuaded to sit higher up by enlarging the hole, together with a little cleaning up of the spring shoes.

BR MINFIT

The Parkside Diagram 1/108 mineral is also available in vacuum-fitted form using the same body parts. Unfortunately, the underframe is for a 10 ft wheelbase vehicle with four-shoe brakegear, whereas *all* BR minerals with 16 ft 6 ins long bodies had 9 ft wheelbase underframes, even the fitted ones, and those built with vacuum brakes had clasp gear except for an early batch of a hundred. Some 1970s conversions were given four-shoe brakes, but retained the shorter wheelbase, and the only vehicles with the longer wheelbase were other 1970s conversions using second-hand 17 ft 6 ins underframes for which new longer bodies were built.

However, a photograph of Minfit B 556306, brand new in Llangollen goods yard in about 1957, spurred me on to unearth a Chivers Finelines etched kit for a standard mineral underframe; admittedly this is for an unfitted wagon, but at least the wheelbase was correct, and information on the layout of the clasp-braked version could be gleaned from the two standard works on BR wagons. Bending up the etched chassis was straightforward using nothing more sophisticated than a pair of smooth-jawed pliers, and then running a fillet of solder into the angles to stiffen it up, taking care to avoid locations where additional fittings were going to be needed. In particular the outriggers which support the body beneath each of the vertical side-members are susceptible to being caught and bent during handling, and a strengthening blob of solder at the inner end of each one is advisable. I also ran some solder along the outer top edges of the headstocks to try to hide the bend line, which is on the outside in this case and consists of an otherwise rather tell-tale series of holes and half-etched spaces between them.

The kit is designed to be constructed in compensated form, the rocking unit

Only the body survives from the Parkside plastic kit for the BR fitted mineral wagon. Everything below that is in brass or white metal, except for a few embellishments like the brake changeover lever attached to the solebar above the V-hanger.

pivoting by the single tab-and-slot method. I have my reservations about this system: I found it tricky to twist the tab sufficiently to all-but-eliminate the tendency of the unit to turn fore and aft whilst at the same time allowing it to rock freely up and down. No doubt a little bit of float in all directions is acceptable, but it seems to me that the method adopted by the EM Gauge Society and D & S, among others, of pivoting the unit about a shaft running lengthways through bearing points at each side is more precise in operation and smacks of better engineering principles.

My other, and perhaps more serious, quibble with the underframe is that, once bent up, both the fixed and floating axleguards are rather too close together to accept standard 26 mm pinpoint axles. A check with a ruler showed that the clearance between the rear faces of the solebars worked out at about 23.5 mm (5 ft $10\frac{1}{2}$ ins) instead of the normal 25 mm (6 ft 3 ins), which naturally had a corresponding effect

on the gap between the W-irons, and one that was too great to overcome merely by bending them outwards. The only solution was to shorten a pair of axles; not the first time I have had to do this, but not a step to be undertaken lightly when you haven't got a lathe at your disposal and have to resort to filing. So I removed one wheel from each axle, filed the pinpoint down by about a millimetre at that end, and then reprofiled the axle by filing a series of flats all round the end at approximately the right angle so that the new point would be as nearly as possible in the centre. I then gradually rounded the flats away and tidied up the pinpoint – which was hardly the precision effort I had just wilfully destroyed, but with a bit of trial and error would pass muster without causing the wagon to limp noticeably and without unduly impairing its free running.

From this point on, modelling the wagon with fitted brakegear complicates the job considerably. It would have been

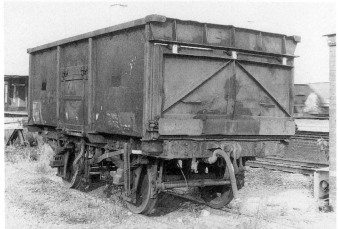

B554826 was built with vacuum brakegear from new in 1958. When photographed at Barnetby in 1991 it was clearly near the end of its life, but, apart from some missing parts, the underframe is in original condition. The body has been reconditioned at some time, however, and reversed on refitting, losing its top flap doors in the process. Subsequently, holes have been cut in the sides to prevent overloading with spent ballast.

far easier to use the parts provided in the underframe kit (two V-hangers, two levers and guards and one two-shoe brake assembly) to make a standard Diagram 1/108 unfitted vehicle, but as it was, only the lever guards were usable for the fitted version. The geometry of the linkage used with BR clasp brakes is far from straight-forward, and even with the etched parts now available from Masokits and a drawing in *An Illustrated History of BR Wagons*, a number of dry runs was necessary to get the location and angle of the various components right. It pays to try to put the linkage together without soldering it up until you're satisfied that it fits and looks right. This is easier said than done, but the first steps are to fix the offset V-hangers in place, the holes cleared to accept a cross shaft of $\frac{1}{32}$ in brass wire, and to bend up the levers and guards and solder them together. Now the levers can be drilled to accept wire pivots at the fulcrum, which is a foot or so from the end of the lever, and also right at the end where they are attached to the slotted lifting links. The end of the arm attached to the link is drilled to fit onto the end of the cross shaft where it protrudes from the V-hanger. Now attach to the solebar the small plate bracket that provides the pivot point for the lever on one side about two feet away from the corresponding V-hanger; on the other side the lever pivots on a horizontal cross-piece joining the two arms of the V-hanger itself. At this stage the wire pivot pins should not be soldered into more than one of the components to allow fine adjustment of the shape of the lever and the angle of the lifting link. To reduce the number of loose bits, however, solder in the cross-shaft remembering to install the two vacuum cylinders at the same time. I used Kenline ones which come complete with operating crank, making one less part to attach, but necessitating some fine tweaking to get the crank to fit the cross shaft and the cylinder to sit squarely on the floor. I filed flats on the rounded tops of the cylinders to assist in this; as built the cylinders were slightly off centre away from the door-end, with the V-hangers offset towards that end about a foot from the centre-line, but it was common in later days to see refurbished wagons with the bodies reversed. Only when you're happy that everything looks right should you fit the lever assemblies and solder it all up.

RCH axleboxes from MJT are a fair match for the BR ones fitted to these wagons, provided that the face of the top part of the casting which the spring sits in is filed flat. A certain amount of filing of the well behind it is necessary at the rocking end to enable the axlebox to clear the spring at maximum up and down deflection. At the other end I used combined axlebox and spring castings of the same pattern.

Clasp brakes came from ABS, and at the compensated end were mounted on the rocking unit itself, which necessitated filing about a millimetre off the base of the mounting block to which each pair of brake shoes is attached. Before fixing, the centre pivot of each shoe was drilled $\frac{1}{32}$ in to accept brass wire yokes – blind holes are cast into the backs of the shoes to help with this. Strictly speaking, the yokes should be in the shape of a flattened triangle, but apart from the fact that you can see something joining the shoes on some photographs (and only the outer ones at that), this detail is generally quite invisible on the real thing. Finally four sets of safety loops were bent up in 26 swg nickel silver wire and soldered to the rocking unit at one end and to the floor at the other: hopefully the shape of these is evident from the photograph, because my vocabulary isn't up to describing it.

Finishing details include MJT 2 ft heavy duty buffers (which to me look quite out of proportion, but are nonetheless correct), vacuum pipes from paperclip wire, spring stops epoxied to the underside of the solebars, and approximations of the brake changeover levers similarly attached beneath the solebars between the arms of the V-hangers. This shows up well in the frontispiece of *An Illustrated History of BR Wagons*, at least well enough to enable a fair representation to be knocked up in styrene. The purpose of the gadget was apparently to apply a differential braking force according to whether a wagon was running loaded or empty.

This view of the completed underside of the fitted mineral illustrates how complicated they are – and the model is a much simplified version of the original! Bits and pieces from eight different manufacturers, plus a number of homemade parts, have gone into it. The rocking axleguard unit (note the slot-and-tab pivot in the centre) is the one further from the camera; at that end the clasp brake castings and wire safety loops are attached to the unit, rather than to the floor at the nearer end.

Right: Another distinctive variety of steel mineral wagon was the so-called 'French' type, built after World War 2 for service overseas but returned to this country in the early fifties. They lacked end and bottom doors, and the cupboard side doors led to their being branded as shown after open ones had been struck by passing trains. Although unfitted, many had screw couplings and longer buffers. The model was scratchbuilt before the release of the Parkside kit. WESSEX COLLECTION

GWR 20-TON MINERAL

I mentioned in the preamble to this section that high-capacity coal wagons were numerically very inferior to those of 16 tons and less until quite recent times. Seventy years ago, however, under the leadership of its General Manager, Sir Felix Pole, the Great Western had made a concerted effort to introduce larger vehicles into its share of the coal trade, to the extent that that gentleman's name became synonymous with the company's distinctive 20- and 21-ton steel wagons throughout their life.

Colin Ashby's plastic kit, originally marketed under the Ian Kirk label, represents the first diagram, N23, with one central side door and doors at each end. Later versions had two doors per side, and some N23s were modified to a three-door layout. The kit could be adapted to either of these, although more easily to the latter; the two-door version is in any case available in etched form from Blacksmith

W110226 and W110437 were both built to the diagram represented by the Colin Ashby kit. The former has had some riveted repairs to the plating at some stage in its life, while the latter has been uprated to 21 tons, but on both wagons the end-door fastening is similar to that featured in the kit. This differs from published drawings and from photographs of other N23 wagons as built (e.g. 110045, 110265) as well as W110019 as running in BR days. At least one of the three-door rebuilds (W33345) had the same fastening as the kit after nationalization, however, so this was perhaps an in-service modification applied to certain members of the class.
ROYE ENGLAND

Models. The three-door rebuilds were in fact intended as loco coal wagons, but unmodified vehicles were also used for this traffic, as witness W 110019 pictured in *Great Western Wagons Appendix*. This was actually the only photograph I found at the time of one of these vehicles in original condition in BR days, although to judge from the fact that the tare weight is still in GWR italic script style, it was taken not long after nationalisation.

The first thing that struck me on looking at the parts was how relatively thin the sides are for a plastic kit; true they are still a shade overscale, but by comparison with Parkside's and Cambrian's clumping great things, they look positively delicate. A pity, then, that the rivet detail is rather heavy-handed, leading to compromises in the number and distribution of rivet heads. And the insides are totally plain, except for some rather unprototypical raised locating strips for sides, ends and floor – rebates would have been better. More significantly, perhaps, the end door fastenings don't match any of the photographs I found of the earliest wagons as built, nor the drawing in *GWR Goods Wagons*, although W 110226 pictured here and some of the three-door rebuilds certainly had end doors of the same pattern as the kit. The difference is that on the early vehicles the fastening bars extend beyond the sides, closing over lugs bracketed to the sides themselves. This requires the ends of the bars to be removed with a sharp blade beyond the edge of the outer vertical straps on the doors, and to be replaced with new ones in 15-thou plastic shaped as a stem matching the width of the locking bar with a rounded head about 1.5 mm in diameter, and long enough to project one millimetre clear of the corner. The stout lugs each comprise two pieces of 20-thou square strip, 'turned' into rod with a file; that part of the lug fixed to the wagon side has a slight flat filed on one side to provide a better mating surface on the short vertical strip of 5-thou representing the brackets above and below. It also has the end nearest the centre of the wagon 'streamlined' – this is better done after the piece has been fitted behind the head of the extended locking bar, and the joint has set properly. The outer end of the lug is the other bit of 20-thou strip filed to a rounded point (before cutting it off the rod) and attached to the front face of the bar. Pins and chains may be added to taste.

The completed N23 mineral wagon, showing end-door modifications, and additional relief work on the reversed brake moulding on this side.

Actually, looking at the photograph of W 110019, I have a feeling that the locking bar should be slightly wider and a bit higher up, but I left it as it was, and just added small strips of 10-thou to represent the way in which the vertical straps are kinked to bridge over the horizontal bar, which also has two 6 mm long grab handles mounted upon it, fashioned from 32 swg brass wire. There is also an additional row of rivets up the extreme edge of the end doors on each side.

A number of compromises have been made with the underframe. I filed the axleboxes and three-leaf (!) springs off the axleguards, substituting RCH boxes from MJT for the former and D & S nine-leaf springs for the latter. In fact, the real thing had seven-leaf ones, but I couldn't find any of those, and unless my old eyes deceive me the D & S castings actually appear to have eight leaves, which I

decided was close enough. These wagons had horn blocks bolted to the face of the axleguards, so I represented these with squares of 10-thou, which I drilled 2 mm to accept the bearings before attaching the new axleboxes. Despite choosing deep bearings, the solebars had to be set out by more than a millimetre to accept 26 mm pinpoint axles; I did this by sticking 25 thou's worth of packing behind each solebar at the point near each end at which they butt up against the raised spacers moulded onto the underside of the floor. The solebars themselves are also a bit shallow, so I put 10-thou packing longitudinally between them and the floor. This in turn meant that the brakegear had to be mounted off the floor, but by a greater margin so that the brake blocks lined up centrally with the axles: 20-thou was barely enough, and meant filing down the lower edge of the carrier block so that it didn't protrude below the solebar.

The two sets of brakegear are identical which of course is incorrect for Morton brakes, so I reversed one set (Morton clutch side) and built up some relief work on the shoes and hangers with plastic strip. Safety loops and V-hangers were replaced with metal ones from a Masokits fret, exopoxied respectively into holes drilled in the carrier block and into the floor behind the solebars. Before fitting the brake assemblies, however, I drilled $\frac{1}{32}$ in holes in the central tumblers and V-hangers for a cross-shaft of 30-thou plastic rod; the tumblers in particular are rather narrow, so a wise precaution in such circumstances is to drill a small pilot hole first and then open it out when you're satisfied it's in the centre. If it isn't, work the small drill bit in and out in a pin chuck to centralise it for the larger bit.

Brake levers also came from Masokits, who cater for longer wheelbase vehicles as well as 9 ft and 10 ft ones. The lever guards were rather unusual, arising from the South Walian belt and braces predilection for both toothed rack *and* pin-and-chain. Relying entirely on the one or two photographs which show this arrangement at all clearly, I cut the toothed rack from a Masokits etching and soldered it down its back edge to the head of a T-shaped piece cut and filed from the surplus metal of the fret. Because the toothed rack is offset both to the right and behind the line of the lever guard proper, this soldered joint must be rather sharper than a right-angle, and the stem of the T bent slightly at its junction with the head to compensate for this before it is soldered behind the guard and the surplus cut off.

Before fitting the combined brake lever and guard assemblies, the four stanchions on each side were extended in the form of L-shaped brackets cut from a sheet of 10-thou, mounted on squares of 5-thou attached to the solebars, and rounded when dry on the outside corner, to make the underframe-to-body supports. The shallowness of the solebars makes these look a bit cramped, but the appearance is improved by comparison with the rather vestigial efforts moulded onto the bottom edges of the sides: the projecting web of these moulded brackets should be removed to give a flush, square base for the upper edge of the horizontal leg of the new brackets to be attached to.

The compromises made with the underframe extend to the omission of spring stops and door springs. The spring stops took the common form of a U-shaped steel bracket bolted to the underside of the solebar. While not quite so simple to make as the solid square or cylindrical cast variety, which are just lumps of plastic strip or rod, they are easy to make in one piece from 30- or 40-thou square strip. With a thin, flat file, or the edge of a V-shaped one, hollow out the end of the strip by filing at an angle, leaving just the very edges of the strip untouched. It doesn't matter what shape the hollow is provided that the visible edges are straight and of constant width. Chop off the last millimetre or so of the strip, and with the open edge uppermost, glue the stop to a short length of 5-thou which you have

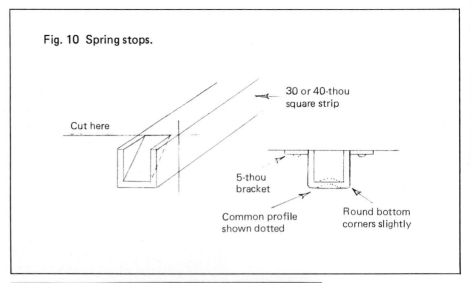

Fig. 10 Spring stops.

Cut here

30 or 40-thou square strip

5-thou bracket

Common profile shown dotted

Round bottom corners slightly

A close-up of the other side of the finished vehicle, highlighting the door springs, the end-door fastening, and the peculiar style of brake guard and rack fitted to some of these wagons.

previously attached beneath the solebar to form the wings on each side. Or, more accurately, stick the stop directly to the solebar and flank it with two small squares of 5-thou.

Reverting to the door springs, these are similar to the ones fitted to the LNER steel open, in that they are bracketed off the face of the solebar immediately behind the projecting door hinges. As before, I soldered a second, L-shaped piece of strip behind the spring proper to produce a spigot to be inserted into a $\frac{1}{32}$ in hole drilled in the solebar immediately above the bottom flange. In effect this gives you the two outer, more visible sides of what I believe is a hollow square bracket bolted to both the solebar and the underside of the floor; the other two sides can be added with plastic strip if you feel so inclined. The outer face of the springs behind and below the door hinges are reinforced with short lengths of plate, some semblance of which is incorporated in the hinge mould-

ings. However, I cleaned the hinges up and replaced the section of plate with strips of 10-thou plastic, sandwiched between the front of the door spring and the back of the hinge. Rivet detail was then applied onto the protruding length of 10-thou below the hinge.

Lastly, I replaced the buffers supplied with ABS 18-inch RCH ones. W 110019 was fitted with buffers with only two short ribs at the sides, so I carved and filed the top and bottom ribs away and shortened the side ones. ABS do in fact make very similar buffers to these which they describe as the BR van and conflat type; being 20 inches long and designed for fitted stock, they are slightly overlength, however. As previously noted, the fat spigots on ABS buffers do pose a threat to the strength of plastic headstocks, and this is especially true here since the ones on this wagon are unusually thin (no more than 25-thou), making it doubly advisable to reduce the diameter of the spigots in this case.

CHAPTER FOUR

HOPPER WAGONS

LNER 20-TON HOPPER

The subject of hoppers is a complex one, and one which in many respects is outside the scope of this book by virtue of their specialised purposes and relatively restricted routeing. Some of the kits for hopper wagons rule themselves out for these reasons; not that there are all that many kits in any case, but LMS coke hoppers and ICI bogie stone carriers are just a bit too recherché to qualify.

One type that I was tempted to omit because of its limited geographical range, but have decided to include on the grounds of the large number built and an extended lifespan of over half a century, is the 20-ton wooden hopper originally designed by the North Eastern Railway at the turn of the century and perpetuated by the LNER. Although largely confined to the North-East, (they did stray into Cumberland as well), they could be seen just about everywhere in that region, being used for the carriage of domestic coal on branch lines as well as coal for shipment and for industry.

Slater's plastic kit is readily available, and comes with copious notes describing the origins and evolution of the species. With a vehicle built over such a long period, it is to be expected that numerous variations on the theme might be found, and my reading of the notes, together with *LNER Wagons*, leads me to the conclusion that the kit represents a wagon built between the end of the Great War and the mid-twenties: that is, between the time when double W-irons ceased to be used and the introduction of standard LNER axleboxes. This is probably an over-simplification, but it typifies the difficulties faced by most of us in trying to build models of vehicles that actually ran in the condition shown, a problem made worse by the realisation that of six sample numbers quoted in the instructions and included on the transfers supplied, the three that can be checked against photographs in *LNER Wagons* belong to vehicles with minor, but noticeable variations to the kit, viz 54143, which has

Slater's LNER 20-ton hopper wagon with the minor modifications described in this section. The left-hand, compensated end is lifted slightly, which exaggerates the gap between the spring and the spring shoes.

crown plates on the solebars (the semicircular strapping above the axleguards); 162100, which has LNER axleboxes; and 182383, which, when photographed in later life, had LNER axleboxes, a deeper central vertical stiffener, and an altered side grab handle arrangement. These are all fairly straightforward modifications, and I opted for 162100, which, as an LNER-built wagon, I reckoned likely to have survived well into the BR period.

Apart from some flash on the mitred corners, the body went together well, the appearance marred only by the plain interior disfigured by impressed moulding marks. The hopper floor was a neat fit, and served to square everything up while the joints hardened. The instructions recommend building the body around the floor, but, especially with an untried kit, I prefer to assemble sides and ends first, at least until I know that the floor is the right size. If it isn't, it's usually easier to adjust the floor than anything else.

I made no alterations to the body of the vehicle other than the addition of label clips (scraps of 5-thou stuck on to a 5-thou backing) which were prominently mounted on the sides, and LNER wagon plates in 10-thou. The kit provides the option of wooden end stanchions for pre-grouping wagons, or steel T-section for those of later build, like 162100. I toyed with the idea of replacing the four main

full-height stiffeners on the sides, which appear from photographs to have been heavier in section than the other strapping, and even to be slightly thicker at the bottom than at the top (like the side-knees of standard RCH wooden minerals), but in the absence of firm evidence I decided to leave well alone. However, I did discard the wire supplied for the handrails these wagons bristled with, since it seemed a bit on the heavy side, and replaced it with finer brass wire of about 11 thou/32 swg, which I find ideal for most similar applications on goods rolling stock. This is obtainable from specialist suppliers, but a good cheap source is the six-strand cable sold for picture-hanging in hardware shops and the like. I recently replenished my stock of this, buying a three-metre length which, when untwisted, gives you about 60 feet of wire for the princely sum of 70 p – enough for several years' modelling at my rate of production.

The moulded parts include a jig for bending up the handrails, but this doesn't take account of the fact that, in common with various other LNER hoppers, the full-width ones across the ends are not quite straight; outside the vertical stanchions on each side they are slightly angled to return closer to the body at their outer ends. They are also bracketed to the stanchions, which on my T-sectioned wagon I represented with short lengths of 10-

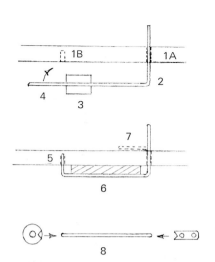

Fig. 11 Making and fitting grabrails.

1A Drill two holes correct distance apart.
1B If rear visible, drill blind holes only.
2   Bend one end of wire and insert in one hole.
3   Grip with pliers just clear of second hole.
4   Remove from first hole and bend second leg; trim to length.
5   For blind holes, coat legs with glue and fit.
6   For clear holes, fit handrail with 20-thou spacer between rail
    and body side.
7   Bend ends over and glue with dabs of epoxy or impact adhesive.
8   Cut brackets from 5-thou strip or 30-thou rounded strip. Cut
    a slight vee and butt up to handrail. Add rivet detail.

thou, chopped out of a sheet with a slightly enlarged, rounded end drilled $\frac{1}{64}$ inch. These were threaded onto the wire before it was finally epoxied into the holes drilled for it, and then Mek-ed to the webs of the stanchions to ensure the handrails were straight (which of course in real life they generally weren't).

In the absence of a jig, the simplest way of bending up handrails is to drill the holes at each end first, bend one end of your length of wire through 90°with pliers, insert that end into one of the holes, and then slide the pliers along until the jaws are almost, but not quite, obscuring the second hole. Provided the wire is bent sharply enough, the two prongs should fit exactly. If the inside isn't going to be visible, these can simply be bent over and dabbed with Evo-stik or epoxy: slide a piece of 20-thou between the handrail and the body side before bending the ends over to make sure it is evenly spaced throughout its length, and leave the spacer in place until the glue sets. If the inner ends would be seen, try to avoid drilling the holes right through, and carefully trim the length of the prongs to achieve the same end.

On the real thing, of course, handrails were rarely fitted quite like this. Usually they were forged into brackets at each end which were bolted to the body. The shape of these brackets varied, being either rectangular or circular as a rule. Rectangular ones can be cut from 5-thou strip, and circular ones from the end of a length of 30-thou square strip, 'turned' with a file. Butted up to the wire, they serve to obscure the unprototypical hole, especially if you cut a slight vee to fit round the end of the wire.

I had decided at the outset to model this wagon in compensated form, and had removed a section of the longitudinal web beneath the floor to accommodate the rocking unit while the floor moulding was still separate. Now I bent up an EM Gauge Society etched RCH W-iron set and fitted it to its pivot cradle with a length of wire of suitable diameter, taking care to ensure that it moved freely, but without undue play. Because the design provides two bearing surfaces, one at each side of the baseplate/cradle assembly, any tendency for the unit to turn as well as rock is minimised, provided the holes for the wire pivot are not opened out any more than absolutely necessary. However, I did feel that the surface area of the cradle to be glued to the floor was quite small, so to avoid any risk of it coming adrift in service, I soldered it to a larger square of nickel-silver sheet about 15-thou thick. Even then, to get the correct height, an additional spacer of 40-thou plastic had to be inserted between it and the floor. However, for reasons which will become clear, I attached this spacer to the nickel-silver plate and not at this stage to the floor.

At this point I did a final tilt-test to make sure that the rocking unit would tip freely under its own weight. With the wheels fitted, I placed the body upside-down on a portable flat surface (actually a small table-mat) and put the unit in place. Holding the table-mat at eye level, I tilted it slightly to one side and the other in turn: I reckoned that if the unit rocked repeatedly at an inclination of 5 degrees or so, it was free enough – that is, almost as soon as the axle was tilted off the hori-

zontal. Only when I was satisfied that I'd got everything right did I solder the wire pivot in place (with the merest touch of the iron at one side to avoid locking the whole thing up solid) and the axle bearings into their holes.

Now I turned my attention to the axlebox and spring assemblies. The style of box fitted to these wagons by the LNER is not, as far as I know, available in 4 mm scale, but I decided it would be fairly easy to modify the NER ones featured in the kit. This means sacrificing the rather nice, and perfectly legible, lettering on the face of the box, which needs to be filed flat and angled inwards towards the top. I cut four blanks in 10-thou to the portly shape of the later design, judged from the photographs in *LNER Wagons*, and stuck these to the now plain face, chamfering the top edge when dry, and adding the more obvious detail such as bolt heads – but not, alas, the replacement cast lettering. This is, I confess, a less than totally satisfactory solution, since the shape of the axlebox proper doesn't exactly match the new overlay; once painted and dirtied, however, I suspect that this will be virtually undetectable if you're not looking for it.

The fixed axleguards can now be fitted to the solebars; I left the axle bearings loose as usual in case I had to change them to give the correct end float in the wheelset, but in fact I didn't. At the other end I filed the axleguards away from the axlebox/spring mouldings, and cut through the springs at the point where they meet the spring shoes. The shoes should only be glued to the underside of the solebar once the axleboxes have been attached to the axleguards and the rocking unit to the floor; this way, the gaps can be minimised.

However, before the rocking unit can be fitted, the brake gear must be added. These wagons, and the steel hoppers that succeeded them, had an idiosyncratic form of clasp brakes on one side only that involved tie rods between each pair of shoes both in front of and behind the wheels. The ones behind the wheels are omitted from the kit, which is no great pity since they're practically invisible from any normal angle. However, the ones in front of the wheels pass between the wheel and the axleguard, which is a distinct disadvantage at the compensated end since it limits the travel of the rocking unit. One possible solution would be to mount the brakegear at that end on the rocking unit, as with the BR Minfit; in this case, however, that meant cutting the brake rodding at some point, and I felt it would be difficult to do this inconspicuously and without making the brakes more vulnerable to handling damage.

So I fixed the brakegear to the floor, first filing down the carrier between the brake shoes at the compensated end to leave room for the rocking unit. Incidentally, having fitted the V-hangers and enlarged the holes to take a $\frac{1}{32}$ in cross shaft (the wire that I felt was too thick for the handrails is rather too thin for this), I found that the brakegear pivoted slightly on the cross-shaft, and had to put a 10-thou packing piece between it and the floor. While the joint was setting I tried to adjust the lateral position of the brakes at the compensated end to make sure that the shoes would line up with the wheel and that the tie rod was more-or-less centralised between wheel and axleguard. This is at best an approximate business, and fine tuning must be left until the rocking unit is finally glued to the floor – hence the reason for fixing the plastic spacer to the unit, which can then be adjusted minutely and only glued by flooding with Mek once it's in the right position.

In the event a gap of almost 1.5 mm between the face of the wheel and the axleguard was enough to permit about three-quarters of a millimetre of up and down deflection of the rocking unit before either wheel or axleguard contacted the tie bar, which I reckon is enough to cope with most track irregularities, at least until someone goes in for faithfully modelling the switchbacks of the average colliery yard, where humps and bumps, angled rail

Two further views of the completed kit, showing the rocking unit and the limited amount of travel allowed it by the brake rodding passing between the wheel and the axleguard.

joints and variations in gauge are practically *de rigueur*.

The brake lever and guard assemblies I fitted as supplied, except for thinning down the top rear edge of the lever to make it less obvious that it was glued flat to the body side. The guards are very plain, and being conspicuous would repay replacement with metal ones. However, other manufacturers would do well to study Slater's turned steel buffers, which are a tight push fit into plastic guides moulded onto the headstocks, and in appearance are definitely a cut above the standard usually supplied with plastic kits.

LNER 13-TON HOPPER

Less well-known than the 20-ton hopper, but rather more widely-travelled, was the 13-ton vehicle, of which three distinct variants were produced by the LNER. One was similar to its larger cousin with sloping sides, another was more akin to a standard RCH mineral, with flat sides but without side or end doors, while the third was somewhere between the two, a sort of half-and-half version with only the bottom two planks on each side sloping inwards. All had a 10 ft 6 ins wheelbase and wooden solebars, and the third variety continued to be built in this archaic form into BR days.

Examples of all three types survived into the sixties, eventually drifting into traffics other than the coal for which they were built, and turning up in some rather odd places. In 1959 several, including E 165182, E 181021 (flat sides) and E 204086 (half-and-half), were to be found carrying stone in the West Country, and were even branded 'Return to Frome W.R.'; in 1960 E 189904 (flat sides) was in use for limestone in County Durham; two years later

E 244347 (half-and-half) was taking iron ore from Immingham to Scunthorpe; and in 1966 E 266572 (sloping sides) was loading coal in Somerset, branded 'Return Empty to Kilmersdon Colliery, Radstock West, W.R.'. Yet others have been noted in Scotland and the West Midlands, so it didn't seem out of place to have the odd one carrying limestone or iron ore in East Denbighshire around 1958; in the absence of a kit, I decided to scratchbuild one of the half-and-half type, a line drawing for which appears in *British Railways Wagons* – the only drawing I've seen for any of the three variants. Photographs of all three appear in *LNER Wagons*. Initially I proceeded very much as I would for any wooden-bodied open wagon. Ignoring the angled hopper sides, I marked out the two sides and ends over the full height on a sheet of 30-thou plastic; this scales out at $2\frac{1}{4}$ inches thick, which is as close as you can reasonably get to the $2\frac{3}{8}$ inches of the original. The depth of the headstocks should be included with each end, but these will need to be thickened up later.

Using a scraperboard knife, I then scribed the planking on both sides of the plastic; this is very much easier if the body sides and ends are marked out on a single base line, so that each one marries up to the one next door, and each plank division can be scribed as a single continuous line. I've already expressed my reservations about mitred corners, and in the interests of preventing that common disease of scratch-built wagons, the tendency of the sides and ends to pull inwards, have suggested avoiding them, and counteracting any misbehaviour in the model by inducing an outward bow before assembly. But remember, if you're going to use butt joints, to allow for the thickness of the sides when marking out the ends (or vice-versa), and unless they're hidden by corner plates, as they are on this particular wagon, to scribe the continuation of the planking on the exposed ends once the body is assembled.

Now you can separate the four parts and thicken up the headstocks by means of a second lamination of 30-thou behind them. Cut the bottom two planks away from the sides and chamfer either or both of the edges of the cut so that the two pieces can be mated snugly again at the right angle; this can be judged against the ends which you will have marked out according to the drawing, and trimmed to shape when cutting out the four parts.

Clearly it will be rather easier to do this once the sides and ends have been assembled, especially if the sides are made to fit outside the ends, which seems the natural way to do it.

Before detailing the body, cut out the solebars from 60-thou, and fit these so that they are slightly inset from the end faces of the headstocks and the bottom edge of the sides – but no more than the 30-thou thickness of the sides to ensure that you've got some kind of joint between the two. Using 60-thou again, cut and fit the three transverse and one central longitudinal members that make the frames of the hopper doors. Once these joints are dry, you have a fairly rigid box on which to apply the external detail; although you can of course do this at almost any stage in the proceedings, there is an obvious difficulty with these wagons in trying to do it before you have determined the angle of the hopper sides. Most of the detail (corner plates, side strapping, and the flat part of the T-section end verticals) is in 5-thou, with the web of the T-section in 10-thou for a little extra strength. The strapping on the sides is of two widths according to the photographs, the verticals being about 2 ins wide whereas the diagonals are about 3 ins. The diagonals overlap the verticals at their lower end and the corner plates at the top, and need to be cranked slightly before fitting to achieve this. Having fitted

the verticals and the corner plates first, lay the diagonal in position and mark on it the two lines of overlap at their correct angle. Hold the outer end of the strip with a pair of plain-jawed pliers, close up and parallel to the first line; grip the plastic between two finger-nails along the line and firmly displace the strip slightly downwards. This should do the trick – at least, it works for me. Repeat for the other end, and attach with solvent.

Handrails and brackets, including the horse-hooks on the solebars, are made as described for the 20-ton hopper. Apart from the horse hooks, detail on the sole-bars consists mainly of prominent washered bolt heads and nuts, which deserve some attention since the solebars are concealed in shadow far less than on an ordinary wagon. So I made the washers in the same way as circular handrail brackets – chopped as thinly as possible off the end of 30-thou rounded strip. The bolt heads came similarly from 20-thou rounded strip, and remaining 'rivets' on the solebars, sides and ends from 10-thou square strip, except that I left riveting the sides and ends until I had finished handling the wagon during the next phases of construction.

At this stage I decided to complete the interior. What I should have done first was to cut and fit on top of the solebars, and on the ledges formed by the thickened

Hopper wagons in the process of receiving iron ore at Immingham Dock in 1962. Apart from some useful detail of the two wagons nearest the camera, the photograph shows one of the LNER 13-ton wooden vehicles with partly-sloping sides. E244347 is in standard BR livery for the period – unpainted woodwork with mere traces of light grey paint adhering to the otherwise rusty ironwork.

headstocks, two pieces of 40-thou to provide a firm base for the axleguard units. But I didn't think this far ahead, and had to wangle them in from underneath after I'd fitted the hopper sections above them. Now the drawing shows the internal layout in outline, but I would have found this difficult to interpret had it not been for a photograph in *Through Countryside and Coalfield* which quite by chance shows a trio of these wagons in a rather distressed state following a rough shunt. One of them is in fact up-ended, revealing extremely useful detail of its inner recesses, which basically consisted of sloping wooden partitions at the sides and ends, those at the sides starting where the outer planking is angled inwards and pitched at round about 45 degrees, and the end ones beginning three planks down and falling at a slightly shallower angle to the top of the outer transverse cross-members. Coupled with the drawing, which confirmed the dimensions and angles, the picture explained everything. Everything, that is, except how the four bottom doors were actually secured and released; this would, perhaps, be gilding the lily, since the underside of the hopper is all but invisible. It presumably has something to do with the two prominent 'horns' below the solebars on each side, which I take to be handles or levers of some sort, and which I represented by filing and bending to shape four lengths of n/s strip, leaving a flat tongue which I glued to the underside of the hopper doors.

These vehicles also present some problems in the underframe department. Apart from the need already identified to build in an element of flat surface on which to mount the axleguard units, (together with appropriate packing pieces – about 80-thou in this case, using EM Gauge Society RCH etchings), the relatively unusual 10 ft 6 ins wheelbase, together with the shape of the hopper bottom, complicates the selection and fitting of brakegear, which, ready-made, tends to come in whole foot sizes. One solution might be to lengthen some plastic 10 ft brakegear (which unfortunately you can't buy separately), and to file away the top edge of the carrier at an angle to suit the hopper sides. The presence of the central cross-beam makes the lengthening process more difficult than previously described, but my inclination would be to cut the carrier as before, separate the two halves by the necessary amount, (presumably 2 mm or

a bit more), and rejoin them with a flitch plate of 40-thou which should be notched to mate with a corresponding notch in the cross-beam. The geometry would need studying, but I see no reason why this shouldn't work.

What I actually did was to solder up some Masokits 10 ft etchings, lengthening the pushrods in the process. This simple statement belies the supreme awkwardness of both operations, and the advice in the instructions to brush up on your grasp of naughty words is not misplaced. Each pushrod consists of three separate bits of brass sheet: two identical sides and a longer packing piece that folds in two and is soldered between them. What I did was to cut each of the sides in two, take the ends which fit round the brakeblock and, holding everything in a pair of pliers, solder them to the packing piece, making sure that they matched exactly for length by running a bit of 26 swg wire through the holes by which the rod will later be attached to the brakeblock. I then repeated the operation for the opposite ends, running a length of finer wire through the adjuster holes, and leaving a one millimetre gap in the centre which I filled up with blobs of solder. Because it has to be done in a hurry so as not to unsolder everything, this is a bit of a hit-and-miss process, and looks untidy until you file the lumps back; with any luck, there will be

enough solder on one side or the other to fill up the space completely between the halves of the pushrods, and not leave unsightly depressions.

Fortunately, these wagons had Morton two-shoe brakes, which meant that I only had two rods to adjust in this way. As for the rest of the assembly, if you proceed methodically according to the instructions you won't go far wrong. Pieces of wire are used to hinge the joints between brake-shoes and pushrods, and between pushrods and tumbler, and I found it useful to pin these five pieces to my all-purpose sheet of balsa by the wires themselves in order to adjust the assembly for length and squareness before soldering up the joints and trimming off the surplus wire. Even so, I suggest that the brakegear should be made and fitted first before the wheels, in order to ensure that the shoes are as close to the tyres as possible – or, at least, that the wheels are not fitted until the brakes are finished. When planning how the wheelsets should fit, I found it necessary to cut away about 2 mm of the baseplate of the axleguard units to slot them round the outer transverse cross-beams. This removed one of the fold-up hinges of the compensation system, and had I not been building a solid underframe, this would have needed some further thought. There is enough meat left in the baseplate to cut and drill another hinge further in, and the

The underside of the scratchbuilt 13-ton hopper with the Morton brakegear and one wheelset loosely fitted into position. If you can work it out upside-down, you'll see that the brake lever on this side must be the one with the clutch so that the downward movement of the lever pushes the rods towards the wheels rather than away from them. The solebar detail and the framing can be seen, together with the hopper door unit in the foreground.

cradle could be mounted off-centre with a short length of brass tube as a washer to take up the extra float; I would be tempted to proceed along these lines, at any rate, though of course this only holds good for the EMGS design of unit. Compensation of hoppers does tend to present these problems.

Returning to the brakegear, the only way I could see of satisfactorily mounting this on the underframe was to solder the brakeshoe hangers to pieces of angled flat plate that could be glued to the sloping underbelly of the hopper. So I bent the hangers to what I judged was the right angle, trying to make sure that I didn't distort them visibly below the level of the solebar. Having soldered each one to its bit of sheet brass, and twiddled and tweaked it to the exact angle, I made up a couple of safety loops from the same Masokits fret, and attached these to the baseplates as well. Because these were in reality attached to the inside face of the solebar, they actually were visibly angled, so to maintain this I doubled the tops over at almost 180° and soldered the 'tails' to the plates.

For the rest of the brakegear I made up my own parts, having already used the etched ones on something else. I also made up the distinctive, angled end steps that hang from the ends of the solebars. I wasn't confident that these would withstand the rigours of normal service if they were just glued on, so I drilled two holes in the top flange and soldered in a couple of short lengths of wire: the lower end to simulate bolt heads, the upper ends to fit into holes in the solebar/headstock corner to provide a more secure anchorage. (Actually, I drilled one of these holes in the wrong place, which made the step decidedly skew-whiff; so I plugged the hole with a bit of rounded styrene strip and re-drilled it when dry – very accommodating stuff, styrene.)

Axlebox and spring castings came from the EM Gauge Society, and represent the cast style of LNER box, rather than the pressed steel ones that many of these 13 ton wagons were fitted with. Buffers were a mixture of RCH and self-contained ones; MJT's 20 inch heavy-duty BR buffers are a reasonable match for the latter, though very marginally overlength, and perhaps a trifle large in the head.

CATFISH

Departmental vehicles are not a particular study of mine, but if there is one class of hopper wagon where you need no excuse for parking an odd one or two at the end of a siding almost anywhere in the country, they must surely fill the bill. In recent years Cambrian have produced kits for quite a number of BR-period types, including the four-wheel, 19-ton Catfish, 446 of which were built to the kit's design between 1953 and 1958. Unlike the two wooden-bodied designs we have looked at so far, more modern hoppers of steel construction tend to be rather skeletal in layout, revealing far more of the underframe, for instance, in many cases than more traditional vehicles. This complicates things for both kit makers and scratchbuilders, mainly because they can no longer rely on the body to provide most of the strength of the model, having to follow prototype practice more closely by using the under-frame to hold everything together.

So it's very important to make sure that the underframe is as strong and as square as possible. This is not easy with this kit, which depends largely on four rather meagre corner joints between solebars and headstocks, and it pays to file the ends of the solebars square to fit snugly into the recess in the back of the headstocks (at the same time as you remove the very visible mould line along the top of the solebars). As always, each pair of parts should be attached separately and allowed to set, rather than trying to assemble all four at

the same time; a degree of additional rigidity and squareness comes from the short floor sections at each end, even though these don't locate very positively (don't be tempted to sit them on the pegs for the brakeshoe mouldings – the floor should be flush with the tops of the headstocks and solebars). But it's still vital to obey the strictures of the instructions to make sure that the vertical axis of the side-stanchions/axleguards is at right-angles to the horizontal axis of the headstocks.

Despite this care, I found when I mated the two halves of the underframe together that I couldn't quite get rid of a twist somewhere in the assembly which stopped one axleguard touching the floor on a flat surface. Having Mek-ed them together I tried to twist the thing the other way, but without success, and eventually left it overnight weighed down and wedged with an assortment of objects in the hope that it would set square. It didn't, and in the end there was nothing for it but to enlarge one of the bearing holes into an oblong in order to displace the bearing by about a third of a millimetre. Incidentally, if you fit the bearings before assembly as recommended by the instructions, leave them removable: I found I had to trim the raised lip around each hole by about half a millimetre to set the bearings far enough apart to accept standard pinpoint axles without forcing the axleguards out.

The instructions also recommend fitting the brakes at an early stage, but in the interests of getting the shoes as close to the wheels as possible without fouling them, I suggest this is left until the underframe is assembled. Admittedly it's a bit more fiddly, but only with the wheels in place can you judge the spacing accurately, especially since it's necessary to bend the hangers slightly to bring them in at the right angle to the tyre. They are correctly spaced for S4 and EM, but would be a bit too far out for OO. OO modellers are also counselled in the instructions to omit the inner brake yokes because they would foul the wheel flanges, but I'm not sure this is necessarily true. I fitted Romford wheels opened out to EM, and had to do a little filing at the ends of the mouldings to give them clearance; however, the diameter of the plastic OO wheels supplied with the kit was the same over the flanges, and there seems to me to be enough meat left in the plastic to file them back far enough to take the narrower wheels without making them impossibly weak.

The reason given for leaving the inner yokes out is that, set out far enough to clear the flanges, they foul the end plates of the hopper chute. If you leave fitting the yokes until after the hopper, however, you can turn this to advantage by filing the ends just enough to clear the flanges but leaving the centre of the yoke butting up to the end plates, to which they can then be glued. If, in addition, you link the two yokes in the centre by a strip of black plastic, you have a much stronger job which doesn't rely entirely on the rather uncertain butt joints of very limited surface area between the end of each yoke and the back of each brakeshoe.

It has to be said that good, positive joints are not this kit's strong point, although, in fairness, modern hoppers don't offer much help in this direction. Another case in point is the method of securing the one-piece hopper moulding to the underframe, which relies on ten side stanchions, five on each solebar, mating with the corresponding stiffeners on the sides and ends of the hopper, with which they again make fairly uncertain joints. To get the hopper to sit square and level, you have to trim one end pair of stanchions slightly shorter to match the pair at the other end – not to match the three short ones in the middle, in case anyone misreads the instructions like I nearly did. Once you're

These two views of the completed Catfish illustrate the modest alterations and additions made to the kit.

satisfied that the hopper is squarely located, you can add the bracing struts that tie the ends of the hopper to the platforms: those at the vacuum cylinder end fit outside the webs of the centre angle iron stiffeners on the hopper body.

With the kit substantially complete, I set about fitting the wire handrails at the control wheel end that are supposed to match the moulded ones attached to the headstock. The moulded rails are impossibly thick, and although I had tried at the start to file them thinner, I still felt they were overscale. So I replaced them all with 20-thou ($1\frac{1}{2}$ inch) brass wire, drilling out the tops of the two end supports before threading the wire through and carefully bending it to locate in holes in each end of the headstock. The platform-to-hopper handrails are easier to fit, but should be slightly further out than the blind holes moulded into the end platform: according to photographs they were in fact bracketed to the top flange of the solebar. The brackets also faced the other way (towards the hopper) in all the pictures I could find, so I filed the moulded ones off and replaced them with 10-thou strip, at the same time adding those at the top of the same rails, and on the headstock at the ends of the

transverse one. Other minor cosmetic alterations and additions were the fitting of a larger solebar number plate, short extensions to the headstocks, which photographs suggest are wider than the solebars, wire vacuum pipes, and brake safety loops. At the outer end, the loops can be set into blocks of 60-thou attached to the underside of the platforms, but the only location for the inner ones is the underframe cross-members just outside the ends of the chute. These are rather thin, so I stuck four small rectangles of black 20-thou to their outer faces to give a bit of meat to drill into. You can see this bodge if you look for it, but a coat of underframe muck should provide the necessary camouflage.

I was tempted to replace the moulded handwheels (one for the hopper, two for the brakes) with etched brass ones from Bill Bedford. If the moulded ones are a bit chunky, however, and in the case of the hopper wheel, perhaps a bit small too, the etched ones look rather spidery for what are, in fact, fairly hefty bits of kit. I think I shall reserve judgment until they're painted, but for the time being, for once, I'm leaving well alone.

BULK GRAIN HOPPERS

LNER bulk grain hopper E203806 in BR colours. At 22½ tons, these vehicles had a higher capacity than any other grain vans of the period. The line of nuts on the side indicates the shape of the internal hopper.
WESSEX COLLECTION

Another class of hopper vehicle which could be seen in penny numbers in many parts of the country is the bulk grain van. Although they were never all that numerous, their association with things agricultural meant that odd ones and twos could often be seen in the daily pick-up goods on rural branch lines from Devon across to Norfolk and from the Home Counties to the north of Scotland.

The construction of railway-built and owned vehicles spanned the four decades prior to 1960, beginning with convertible wooden vans designed by the GWR and ending with the 20-ton steel hoppers that have only been phased out in the last few years. Although the design changed radically in the meantime, it is interesting to see that certain principal dimensions, including the 10 ft 6 ins wheelbase, remained almost unvaried throughout the period, with the principal exception of twelve steel-bodied vehicles, again produced by the GWR, which were notably shorter than all the others. In fact, these twelve wagons were the only ones to resemble in length (but in no other material way) the well-known ready-to-run product from Hornby Dublo/Wrenn, which was clearly tailored to fit an existing underframe, and has managed to remain 2 ft 6 in undersized ever since.

Only two kits have ever materialized for bulk grain vans: K's white metal kit for the GWR steel-bodied version, and the Parkside one of the distinctive LNER derivative of the GWR's pioneer wooden design. Although examples of both survived into the seventies, they were always in the minority compared with the 800-plus steel hoppers produced initially by the LMS, and later developed by BR. Now there's a well-known law of railway modelling that says that if you build a wagon – any wagon – from scratch today, somebody will produce a kit tomorrow. I've lost count of how many times it's happened to me, but so far steel grain vans are the exception that proves the rule: I've built seven, and I'm still living in hopes.

The rule certainly worked in the case of Parkside's LNER wagon, and with a few reservations and a bit of the usual effort, the kit is good enough for me not to have to scratchbuild any more, as a comparison with the photographs in *LNER Wagons*, and the pictures and drawings in the February 1976 issue of *Model Railway Constructor*, will soon show. Being essentially van-shaped, the kit's construction is relatively straightforward, and the fact that they remained virtually unaltered throughout their lives, livery changes apart, is an added bonus.

Other than the roof (which because of the top door detail is rather unusually injection moulded rather than the normal plain piece of styrene sheet), the construction of vans is not significantly different from the open wagons we have looked at so far. Sides and ends generally fit together in the same way, as does the floor and underframe assembly. Because of their function, however, these wagons present a number of interesting features which placed them apart from the vans they superficially resembled. Internally, in fact, they were quite similar to the 13-ton open hopper described earlier, although this is betrayed only by the nut-and-bolt detail on the sides and ends. Unlike the open wagons, however, the shape of the hopper extends below the solebar and results in brake gear of an unusual design.

The only major omission from the sides and ends is the complete absence of grab handles and handrails. There were five in fact, plus others on the roof, two short diagonal ones at the bottom left-hand corners of the body sides, two for the end steps giving access to the roof, and one on the inspection door half-way along one side. These I represented with my usual 32 swg brass wire, adding fixing brackets of 5-thou strip where they were inserted into $\frac{1}{64}$ inch holes drilled in the mouldings.

(The end handrails can't be fitted, of course, until after the roof goes on.) Incidentally, the only official drawing I have seen of these vehicles, the one reproduced in *LNER Wagons*, shows diagonal rails at both bottom corners of the side, but the right-hand one is absent from all the photographs.

The body-to-solebar brackets are moulded as plain downward extensions of the side strapping, whereas in fact the flat element of the T-section was turned under at the bottom and attached to the top of the lower solebar flange. This can be added in 10- or 15-thou strip after the solebars have been fitted, although it may be necessary to shorten the extensions when you do so. According to photographs, the angle that formed the corner plates tapered to a point below the body side, whereas on the kit it stops short, level with the top of the headstock.

These details apart, the strapping on the sides and ends is nicely done, although the corners of the end vents are unaccountably rounded (which can be remedied inconspicuously by an overlay of 10-thou), and the end steps don't project far enough: I added 1.5 × 3 mm rectangles of 10-thou Mek-ed to the tops of the moulded ones. Lastly, as the notes point out, the end inspection windows, which are blind recesses set into the planking, were plated over latterly, so I added rectangles of 5-thou to simulate this.

The end mouldings are slightly rebated to receive the sides, and some cleaning up is necessary to achieve a good joint. Even so, cosmetically it's difficult to disguise the joint properly on the outside, and the only truly satisfactory solution would be to file away the section of corner plate moulded on the sides and replace it in 5-thou so that it overlaps the half-millimetre or so of the end that's visible beyond the side. This would enable you to extend the corner plate where it tapers off to the bottom of the headstock. Once all four sides and ends are united, the floor can be added, followed by the roof. This is a rather imperfect moulding with some strange undulations near the roof doors, which, however, can easily be filed away. After you have filed them off, finish up with some wet-or-dry to remove any lingering file marks, then give the areas a wash over with a brushful of solvent: this restores the lustre to the surface and prevents you getting a different paint finish on the filed areas from the rest of the roof.

I also removed the detail from the top of the roof doors. I did this mainly because it didn't quite match the two vehicles I had previously scratchbuilt, but also because it is my impression that the doors aren't quite large enough. I say impression because the evidence is contradictory: the drawing in *LNER Wagons* certainly shows them rather longer than on the model, but no end elevation or roof plan are included; the instruction sheet refers to this, and to the drawings in *MRC* which were done from measurements, but which show the doors as slightly shorter than the first drawing, but still some 2 mm longer than the model. On width, however, the model and *MRC* agree, but photographic evidence in the same article suggests to me, at least, that they were a good bit wider, perhaps as much as six inches more. Anyway, whatever the rights and wrongs of it, once I'd filed them smooth, I added an overlay of 10-thou about 2 mm larger all round. According to the photographs, there is in fact an overlap on three sides, the fourth being at the outer end where I take it there was a length of angle to act as a door stop. So against this edge of the door I stuck a piece of 10-thou strip curved slightly to the roof profile.

I then replaced the reinforcing ironwork on top of the door in 10-thou, adding a representation of the locking hasp at the outer end, and of the runner wheel at the inner. This is ignored on the kit, but is not difficult to fabricate using two circles of 10-thou and a slightly smaller one of 20-thou sandwiched between them, plus four lengths of 1 mm wide 10-thou strip for the bracket work attaching the wheel to the end of the door. Lastly, I added the two transverse grab rails between the longitudinal angles, which I judged to be $2\frac{1}{2}$ to 3 mm in from the ends.

I also reckoned the roof to be a bit short, and extended it by sticking a length of 15-

A close-up of the inspection door, brakegear and bottom door gear of the wagon illustrated opposite. On the other side, the brake lever pivots on a smaller V-hanger and acts on the cross shaft via a lifting link. WESSEX COLLECTION

A comparison between the Parkside kit, on the left, and a scratchbuilt model of the LNER grain hopper. Only one side has an inspection door.

thou strip, again curved with the fingers to the roof profile, onto each end, covering the join with a strip of 10-thou across the top as per the photographs. With the roof fitted I drilled fixing holes for the end handrails and the separate roof-mounted grab handles next to them.

Turning to the underframe, when I came to fit the solebars, I noticed that the holes for the bearings in the backs of the axleboxes were all slightly offset; not by much, but enough to set the axles askew unless the solebars themselves are offset to compensate. This involved shortening each solebar at its left-hand end and packing the other end away from the headstock by 15 thou. It was also necessary to play about with the location of the V-hangers on both solebars; these are two identical mouldings, each with one short hanger on the right and a longer one on the left. The instructions correctly tell you to remove the left-hand one from the side with the inspection door, but unfortunately this leaves the short one on this side opposite the long one on the other side. Since the brake cross-shaft ran between them, they should both be long. To make matters worse, they're not quite opposite each other, although offsetting the solebars has brought them slightly closer! So you should (a) cut off one of the short V-hangers and put the long one from that side in its place; and (b) move the long one on the other side about 2 mm to its left. The easiest way to do this is to chop them off immediately below the solebar and re-fix them with the aid of 20-thou strips acting as flitch plates across each new joint at the back. Take it from me that these are next to invisible when painted. Incidentally, you have to move both, rather than just one, because this is where

they have to be on the model (and actually were on the real thing) to enable the cross-shaft to clear the underside of the hopper.

Unfortunately, the end arm of the brake lever that incorporates the lifting link is now too short, so you have to extend it to the length it should be by grafting a couple of millimetres onto the end. If you file away about half the thickness of the arm from the rear, you can then replace this with a strip of 10-thou long enough to extend the extra 2 mm beyond the end. Now stick a 2 mm length onto the protruding section equal in thickness to the thinned-down original, and you have a strong, invisible joint in an arm of the correct length (see *Fig 6*).

I neglected two other possible improvements which seemed less noticeable when

I built the vehicle a year or two ago, but which I would attend to with any future construction: the axlebox and 7-leaf spring assemblies are rather coarsely reproduced, and while the former can be improved rather like the LNER steel open and 20-ton hopper wagons, the latter are really beyond reclamation. D & S 9-leaf springs (the ones with only 8 leaves) would be an

Detail photographs of a scratchbuilt vehicle, showing roof doors, end steps and brake and door gear. The asymmetrical brakegear was made up from brass strip using shoes cut from 40-thou plastic sheet, and the operating wheel from fine wire as described in this section.

acceptable substitute. The other improvement relates to the buffers. These are marginally too short for standard 18 inch ones, and mine were not well moulded, with an offset that would have made them even shorter if I'd tried to get rid of it. ABS RCH unfitted buffers would be suitable. One other embellishment I did include, however, was a representation of the bottom door operating gear. This doesn't show up well on photographs, but it seeems that the door slid horizontally towards the side with the inspection hatch along a guide which at its outer end was connected to a double vertical arm that passed either side of the handwheel cross-shaft. Obviously there was more to it than that, but at least it's not very visible, so I contented myself with fabricating those pieces, and left it at that.

SCRATCHBUILDING A STEEL GRAIN VAN

My first shot at building a steel-bodied grain hopper involved a Wrenn vehicle. I bought it in the full knowledge that the underframe was useless to me and that the body was too short, but at least the shape looked right. As it turned out, that's about its only plus point. By the time I'd carved and filed all the detail off, lengthened body and roof by sawing them down the middle and grafting a 10 mm wide section into the gap, stuck it all back together, redetailed it and totally scratchbuilt a new underframe, I'd come to the conclusion that I might as well have started from scratch in the first place. So that's what I did with the next six.

The immediate problem to be solved in scratchbuilding a steel grain van is how to capture the roof profile. Thinking about it before hand suggested two or three possible solutions. The first, and perhaps the most obvious, was to make it like a van or carriage roof: plastic sheet up to 15 or even 20-thou thick can be curved very easily by laying it across the join of two overlapping sheets of cardboard and rubbing vigorously along the line of the join with a smooth, rounded tool – the handle of an ordinary table knife, the sort with a bone or plastic handle, is ideal. This induces a gradual curve if repeated all the way across the width of the plastic, suitable for the single-arc roofs fitted to early carriages and most goods vans. For a triple-arc roof the tighter curve at the sides can be made by drawing the point of a centre punch along a straightedge, again on a

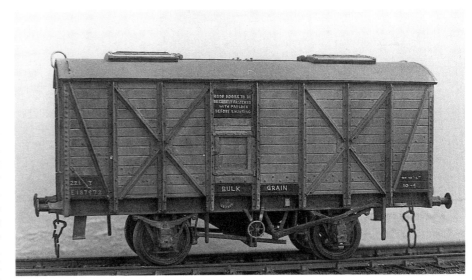

A second scratchbuilt LNER van. Note the various different wordings of the instructions about the roof doors. The axleboxes and springs, adapted from castings for ordinary ones, don't do full justice at close range to the heavy-duty fittings on the original.

The last 100 grain hoppers built to Diagram 1/271 were vacuum-piped; although fitted with hand brakes only themselves, they could be marshalled between fitted vehicles without impairing the automatic brakes of the ones behind them. For this reason, they were painted in bauxite livery. B885634 has a lengthened Wrenn body, but is otherwise scratchbuilt, including the roller-bearing axleboxes.

sheet of card; the closer the intervals between the lines, and the harder you press, the sharper will be the radius of the resulting curve. In 10-thou plastic, a radius of 4 mm is quite feasible. Don't use anything with a pin-point, because this will tear the surface; as it is, the point of the punch will leave a series of lines or ridges on the outside, and for this reason when using this method on thin material I generally prepare two pieces in the same way and then glue them together. Laminating in this way not only gives you enough thickness to be able to file the ridges away, but it ensures that the curves will be held, and won't be able to straighten themselves

out. To make assurance doubly sure, fit the pre-curved roof over a series of formers profiled to the inside radii and stuck on edge to a flat false ceiling. Three formers should be enough for a fairly short vehicle. Laminate three thicknesses of material (say, 30-thou) for the false ceiling as shown in the diagram to provide rebates for both the roof and sides to sit in, and, when set, smooth the joints over with file and wet-or-dry.

An alternative, though to my mind rather long-winded, way of producing a roof in plastic is to soften the material with heat over a pattern block – long-winded because first you have to make the pattern,

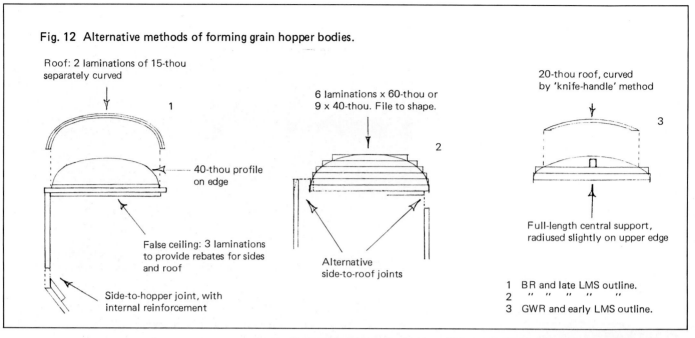

Fig. 12 Alternative methods of forming grain hopper bodies.

Roof: 2 laminations of 15-thou
separately curved

40-thou profile
on edge

False ceiling: 3 laminations
to provide rebates for sides
and roof

Side-to-hopper joint, with
internal reinforcement

6 laminations x 60-thou or
9 x 40-thou. File to shape.

Alternative
side-to-roof joints

20-thou roof, curved
by 'knife-handle' method

Full-length central support,
radiused slightly on upper edge

1   BR and late LMS outline.
2   "   "   "   "   "
3   GWR and early LMS outline.

and unless you're batch-building lots of identical vehicles, it hardly seems worth the effort.

In fact, I chose a third method which seemed to offer both solidity and more controllable results: filing the whole thing from the solid. Again the diagram shows the principle: laminate together six thicknesses of 60-thou, making sure by prising each leaf apart progressively as you add the solvent, that as far as possible the liquid goes everywhere leaving no dry spots. Leave for at least 24 hours, preferably longer, before filing to shape using coarse files to start with, then finer ones, and finally wet-or-dry. When you're sure you've got the size and shape right, add a further lamination of 30 or 40-thou underneath, narrower by 2 mm to provide a rebate for the tops of the 40-thou sides, and when these have been added, smooth down the final part of the curve. Actually, the number of laminations and the order of the various jobs are not all that critical: you may find it easier to extend the sides upwards and set them outside the laminated lump, or to put the sides and ends together first and drop the raw roof in afterwards, and then file to shape. The important thing to remember is to build enough meat into the joints to make sure that the body remains strong when you've finished.

The diagram also shows a third possible method which is a sort of cross between the two, and would be suitable for the different roof profile of the GWR and early LMS steel vehicles. In this case, lami-

A comparison between the ends of BR and early LMS-built vans highlights the difference in body profile and the layout of the underframe members. BR used welded construction for the most part, while the LMS favoured riveted steelwork; the rivets are 'floated' on individually in the manner described in Chapter 2 under the heading of the GWR open wagon.

nation provides the quite sharp bend at the eaves (for want of a better word), and 'knife-handle' curving the flatter profile of the centre section.

The basic shape of the body is completed by the addition of the hopper section. The geometry of this is fairly complex, but essentially it consists of four sloping, tapering sides falling to a narrow, 15 inch square hatch at the bottom. The ends of the hopper should be sized to fit inside the ends and sides to avoid the risk of unsightly joints, and the hopper sides must make an angled joint with the ver-

tical sides just above the solebar. For all that I've said about mitre joints, there isn't much alternative here, but you might try reinforcing it with a strip of 30 or 40-thou stuck to the inside of one piece or other so that it overlaps by 2 mm or so, chamfering the projecting edge to fit behind the other section, making an interlocking joint.

Details of these various profiles can be found in drawings published in *A History of GWR Goods Wagons*, *An Illustrated History of LMS Wagons*, *The LMS Wagon*, and *British Railways Wagons*. Curiously, there seems to be no drawing of the most common of the lot, BR Diagram 1/271, which accounted for 570 vehicles, over two-thirds of the total, but these are in fact very similar in all major respects to the drawing of 1/270 in *British Railways Wagons*, except that the external angle-iron stiffening was no longer carried over the roof, but stopped at the top of the sides. The external angle was a feature of all the LMS wagons, and is really the only tricky job to do in detailing the body of any of these vehicles. The projecting web of the angle needs to be curved to the roof profile before it is stuck on. Narrow 10-thou strip can be bent quite sharply across the flat with a pair of plain-jawed pliers; bit-by-bit, working round the whole radius of the curve, grip the plastic with the pliers and with your other hand pull the strip gently to one side. If you don't try to achieve too much too quickly, you'll be surprised how sharp a bend you can get before it breaks.

Positioning of the projecting web is a lot easier if the flat part of the angle has been attached first. Because this extends down to the upper edge of the hopper section, then turns in, and then down again over the solebar, clearly the solebar needs to be fitted before the side strapping. Which brings us onto the underframe.

Underframe details for most of these wagons are not easy to establish, and the modeller's task is not made easier by the fact that they were almost all different, and at least partly visible beneath the elevated ends. Only one of the sources listed earlier boasts an underframe drawing (for the principal LMS design) but, based on my own photographs, most of the BR vehicles were as shown in the sketch. Dimensions are approximate, except for the distance between the solebars; these and all other members were ten inches deep on all designs.

Except for the solebars, which are made as described for the BR Medfit, all other underframe sections, including the head-stocks, were made from 60-thou plastic the fact that it isn't channel section is invisible once painted. For extra strength I filled in the angle of the corner posts between the ends of the body and the headstocks with 30-thou square strip, one corner of which I bevelled so that it would not be too conspicuous inside the angle. With the solebars fitted, I could now put on the side stiffening, filling in the gap between the flat part of the angle and the face of the solebars with noggins of 20-

The elevated angle of this photograph of an early van built to Diagram 1/271 offers some useful information on the roof door layout and on the method of construction of the area beneath the overhanging end. WESSEX COLLECTION

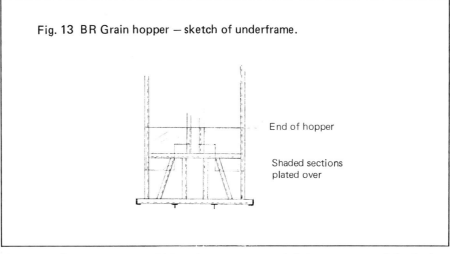

Fig. 13 BR Grain hopper — sketch of underframe.

End of hopper

Shaded sections
plated over

thou to make a strong joint. Although, as I've said, it's possible to bend 10-thou strip for the web to the radius of the roof, it isn't practicable to induce the sharp reverse angle where the body meets the solebar, so each of these was made up of two separate short lengths of strip, cut to fit the adjacent section(s) and then tidied up with a file and a blade when dry.

Lastly on the body, I made up the end ladders from Colin Waite etched signal ladder kits. It is a great misfortune that these are no longer on the market, because

to my mind they were certainly the best ever. Alternatives are available, but somehow they don't capture the delicacy of the real thing. My method for soldering them up, which would equally apply to others, such as Model Signal Engineering parts, is as follows: glue a small cube of balsa to one end of your balsa block, and gently push the ends of the sides of the ladder into it at the correct spacing. Insert pins at intervals along the length of the ladder to maintain the spacing and the uprightness of the sides, then thread the

The GWR's second style of bulk grain van was a complete departure from its earlier wooden design, and bore all the main features of other varieties of steel-bodied wagon, differing only in overall length and the absence of outside angle-iron stiffening. Only twelve were built.

rungs through the etched holes and solder. Don't solder from one end in sequence, or you may find the ladder distorts as you go; solder opposite ends first, then work in towards the middle from both ends alternately. Make the rungs appreciably overlength to start with, and when finished snip the excess off with a pair of scissors and clean up with a file. Then very, very carefully bend the ends in a bit at a time with the pliers and form brackets to attach to the vehicle. Incidentally, ladders on these wagons were quite narrow, mostly no more than $7\frac{1}{2}$ inches or so, according to the drawings.

When it comes to the running gear, we face another difficulty. The GWR and LMS wagons were fitted with RCH split axleboxes, but with seven-leaf springs, which I think are unavailable commercially: you have a choice between five and nine. More serious, perhaps, is the fact that roller bearings were commonly fitted to the BR-built wagons, and later to some of the older vehicles as well, and that although axleguards to suit are available from the EM Gauge Society, Comet and MJT, neither they nor anyone else has ever produced Timken roller bearing axleboxes of the correct pattern. For the converted Wrenn vehicle I scratchbuilt all four spring and axlebox assemblies, and subsequently for the later wagons had some white metal castings done from my own pattern. One of these days I shall try casting my own.

Fabricating your own springs and axleboxes is not as difficult as you might think, although roller-bearing ones are not the

simplest to make. I started with a plain sheet of 10-thou plastic and built each one up on it, a bit at a time. The springs are cut from 40-thou into which a series of concentric lines denoting the separate leaves have first been scribed with a pair of dividers; as they are cut out, the ends of the leaves are represented by a series of steps in the lower edge. The springs end at the shoes, which are bits of 30-thou stuck to the backing sheet on edge and shaped when dry; tiny offcuts form the projection of the ends of the top two leaves outside them. The key to making the axlebox itself is realising that the backing sheet forms part of the final assembly, in this case the hornblocks on either side of the box. With squarish axleboxes, such as LNER or BR plate-fronted ones, all you need to do is to laminate together two pieces of strip of the correct width, say two by 60-thou by 3 mm wide, or whatever, shape as necessary on the end of the rod thus formed, and chop off at the appropriate length. Details, such as the ribbing for split axleboxes, bolt heads, etc, can be added once the block has been attached to the backing sheet. The spring saddle and the buckle can be filled in with suitably shaped pieces of strip.

As I say, roller-bearing axleboxes are rather more complex in outline, but the principle is the same. Try to break the thing down into as many simple component bits or layers as possible: hornblock, bearing surface, box, circular cover plate, and the inverted U-shaped lip that surrounds it, are each made from different thicknesses of sheet or strip,

roughly shaped before attaching, then delicately filed and scraped. One of the hardest things to reproduce is the two square holes in the top of the casting that housed the standard Timken bearing: I drilled a couple of 0.5 mm holes and then used the tip of the scraperboard knife to angle the corners.

When you're satisfied with the outline, cut round the assembly so that it comes away in one piece, but don't drill the hole in the back until you can judge the correct position with the axleguards in place. Because of the underside of the hopper and the two central longitudinal underframe members, using standard etched axleguard units becomes difficult. Since I was building a rigid underframe, I attached each of the axleguards separately, relying mainly on Evo-sticking them behind the solebars, but leaving also a small tongue bent at right-angles under the plated-in section that partly floors the space under the end of the body. Because this 'floor' is only 10-thou, it doesn't give a lot of additional support to the axleguard, but anything's better than nothing.

Compensating these vehicles would not be easy, and it might be wiser to resort to a bit of slop in the axles. There certainly isn't enough room to use an unmodified etched rocking unit, but you might get away with reducing the depth of the two longitudinals and bridging them to accommodate the cradle, but only at the expense of making a new and much smaller one and altering the shape of the plate between the axleguards, and of cutting a hole in the hoppers. Such a hole would be quite inconspicuous if confined to the area behind the solebars, but because of the see-through nature of the underframe beneath the ends of the body, it would be almost impossible to conceal the rocking unit entirely when viewing the wagon from the end.

Happily, with the exception of the GWR vehicles, which had a rather cramped version of the system fitted to the LNER hoppers, the brakegear on the LMS and BR vans was refreshingly simple. All were handbraked only, except for the final batch of a hundred, which were vacuum-fitted and clasp-braked, and departed from previous designs for the first time by having a longer wheelbase; in addition, the two previous lots were through-piped (and therefore in bauxite livery), but otherwise identical to earlier vehicles. At each end a handbrake lever operated a cross-shaft between V-hangers on both sides which pulled a single pair of yoked brake shoes onto the outer faces of the wheel tyres. The hangers for these shoes were attached at their upper end to the underframe cross-member level with the outermost side stanchion. You may be able to find a spare set of plastic shoes from another project, but if not they are not difficult to cut out of 40-thou sheet in one piece complete with hangers. Add some relief detail to the hanger and curved edge of the shoe, and drill the rear of the shoe to accept a yoke of 30-thou plastic rod.

The levers are made in the normal way, as are the guards, but because these are some way from the nearest axleguard, they are braced by an angled strut from the bottom of the guard to the underside of the solebar. All the steel-bodied vans were fitted with tie-bars between the axle-guards.

The pre-nationalisation designs were fitted with bottom door operating wheels on both sides of the vehicle, but in BR days the one on the non-inspection hatch side was often removed, and most BR-built wagons seem to have only had one. Nowadays a selection of etched wheels of both straight and curly spoked styles is available from Bill Bedford Models, but when I built mine you had to do it the hard way. I started by forcing a piece of 26 swg wire into a balsa block and then winding 32 swg wire tightly round it to make each pair of spokes. Try to compress these together as you solder them all on at the same time with the overlong spokes radiating evenly from the centre. Once they are fixed, adjust the angle of any that

need it and trim to length with a pair of scissors; if you're making a wheel with curved spokes, curve them now, but not too much. Bend up a rim of 32 swg wire, turning one end outwards to make a handle if required, and touch solder to the

ends of the spokes. Despite the fact that the spokes don't radiate from exactly the same point along the length of the shaft, this is only noticeable on very close inspection, and is even less so if you finish by filing the hub of the wheel flat.

Construction of the LMS steel vans began in 1928 and more than a hundred were built over the next twelve years. Most of these had a similar roof outline to the GWR Grano, but with outside angle reinforcement. This particular model uses the axleguard, box and spring mouldings from the old 3H LMS coke hopper kit.

The final ten LMS wagons, and the first 40 BR ones, had a new roof shape, although still with reinforcing angle carried right over the top. To keep within the loading gauge, the web of the angle iron had to be chamfered at eaves level, which gave these vehicles a particularly distinctive appearance.

The majority of the BR-built vans were to the cleaner outline of Diagram 1/271. The roller-bearing axlebox and spring assemblies were cast to my own pattern built up in styrene. They should, however, have seven-leaf springs.

A very helpful elevated view of a standard BR-built shock open with tarpaulin bar, similar to the Parkside kit. Note especially the underframe visible at the end, the unusual longitudinal floor planking (was this normal? — all the drawings in An Illustrated History of BR Wagons show transverse planks), the wooden sheathing inside the corrugated steel ends, the angle of the bottom plank of the side door (reproduced on the inside), and the special buffers (available in cast form from MJT).   WESSEX COLLECTION